Dreams of Fields
Memory Traces of Iowa's Past

DREAMS OF FIELDS

MEMORY TRACES OF IOWA'S PAST

Essays by Roy R. Behrens

Ice Cube Press
North Liberty, Iowa

Dreams of Fields:
Memory Traces of Iowa's Past
© 2025 Roy R. Behrens
Printed and bound in the USA
With recycled paper
1 3 5 7 9 8 6 4 2

Ice Cube Press, LLC (Est. 1993)
North Liberty, Iowa 52317
319-594-6022
www.icecubepress.com

ISBN 9781948509626
Library of Congress Control Number: XXXXXXXXX

The paper used in this publication meets the minimum requirements of the American National Standard for Information Sciences: Permanence of Paper for Printed Library Materials, ANSI Z39.48-1992.

CONTENTS

Introduction / 8

Salvador Dali in Cedar Falls / 12

Ringgold County's Corn Parade / 20

Holding Down the Fort's Remains / 26

A Turbid and Unfriendly Trek / 32

The Riotous Wild West / 38

Hot Frankfurters on Unbuttered Bread / 44

Wilde, Whiskey and the Peacock Room / 50

When Emerson Walked on Water / 56

Sand Painting on the Mississippi / 62

Living Among the Navajo / 68

Searching for Frank Lloyd Wright's Father / 74

A Tale of Twain Wives / 80

Arts, Crafts, Scandal, Sudden Death / 86

Occupant of a House by Le Corbusier / 92

Flatlanders Go Down Under / 100

Sherry Fry and the Birth of Camouflage / 106

Iowa's King of the Realm of the Koin / 112

Sophie Tucker Meets Spirit Lake / 118

Ripley's Ghost Believe It or Not / 126

Ottumwa's Theatrical Ship Camoufleur / 132

The Impresario of Book Design / 138

Horse Racing's One-Time Pooh-Bah / 152

Airborne Version of Buffalo Bill / 158

An Edifice to Expediency / 164

Flotsam Adrift in a Maddening Crowd / 170

End Matter / 177

Dedicated to the memory of
Guy Davenport (1927-2005)
friend and correspondent
whose essays are collected in
The Geography of the Imagination

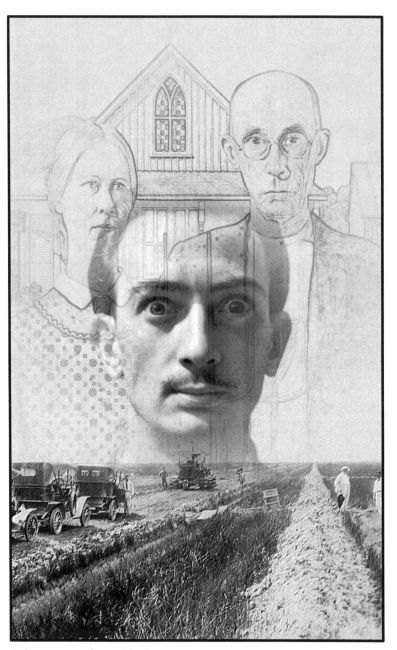

Author's montage from public domain components

INTRODUCTION

ROBERT FROST *Death of the Hired Man*
**Home is the place where, when you have to go
there, they have to take you in.**

IN THOMAS WOLFE'S famous novel, *You Can't Go Home Again*, the main character (a novelist like Wolfe) concludes: "You can't go back home to your family, back home to your childhood... back home to the old forms and systems of things which once seemed everlasting, but which are changing all the time..."

Years later, it may have been artist Larry Rivers who said: "You *can* go home again. But you can't stay longer than forty-five minutes."

I was born in Iowa. I lived there continuously for seventeen years. As Iowa native Jake Johanssen said, "It took a long time for me to realize that we were free to go."

I COULD HAVE claimed that I was born in "rural Iowa." But when I was growing up, all of Iowa was rural. Or, at least, it wasn't urban, and the pace of change was dreadfully slow. My departure was as painful as it was inevitable.

It was painful because, as Helen Hayes explained, everyone of us is "born with the tragedy that he has to grow up...that he has to leave the nest, the security, and go out to do battle. He has to lose everything that is lovely and fight for a new loveliness of his own making, and it's a tragedy. A lot of people don't have the courage to do it."

It was also inevitable. I sensed that if I did not leave, my dreams would start to ossify. I would surely be overwhelmed by complacency and convenience, and my zeal to live life fully would soon begin to falter.

I was reminded of that a few years ago, when I read Bruce Kellner's account of how Carl Van Vechten escaped from the Iowa town in which he grew up.

Van Vechten's birthplace, according to Kellner, "was like one of its [Iowa's] customary midday meals, wholesome and plentiful, unimaginatively but well cooked, on which one might grow. [But] to stick around for second helpings…could induce indigestion: the corn belt had a way of stealthily tightening around the belly."

So, as Kellner concluded, Van Vechten "was born in Iowa, but he got out as soon as possible."

I HAVE to wonder: Did Carl Van Vechten ever look back? We know that Grant Wood certainly did. He left the American Midwest in quest of something greater than the vast cornfields in which he had been quarantined.

But, with much the same disillusion he felt when he initially fled, he turned his back on Europe and came home to view his surroundings anew–through a modified filter–with a tint of intrigue and rich detail that he had only seen abroad before. Some of his best ideas, he said, "came to me while I was milking a cow."

In the years that followed my own escape, I was fortunate to live temporarily in a bewildering sequence of places–among them California, Colorado, Hawaii, Rhode Island, Wisconsin, Georgia, and Ohio. Each place had its treachery. But each was also a source of mystique.

At age forty-five, when I returned to live in Iowa, it was not that I reversed my course. Instead, I came back as an emigré from a crazy quilt of adjacent yet exotic lands–entrenched, still intact pockets of the great American melting pot, outposts that had yet to melt. But, like Grant Wood, I returned with a new set of lenses by which the too-familiar surrounds were once again opened to exploration—as it was when I was young, growing up in Iowa.

A FRIEND OF MINE once said of someone, whom he believed to be shallow, that "if you scratch his surface, you will only come out on the opposite side." For many people, their lasting impression of Iowa is that it is all too dreadfully shallow, despite its boast of deep, rich soil. It is, as is commonly noted, "the flyover state," a region where Flat Earth believers could thrive, a land where, as Iowa-born writer Bill Bryson once said, if you stand on two telephone books, you can see forever.

I had discovered a wondrous approach, as is exemplified by the stories in this book. The simple solution I found was to dig below appearances, to unearth the surface wherever I stand.

The essays here are evidence of the rich remains that one can find by recalling Iowa's peopled past, by searching for its arrowheads. They are not "fields of dreams" as such, but rather more like *dreams of fields*. And what better dreams could one hope for than those that restore the achievements of remarkable characters from the past who were born in Iowa. Or who lived here. Or who maybe just stopped by to talk.

I conclude with a favorite story: In the early 1990s, the New York mobster Salvatore ("Sammy The Bull") Gravano agreed to cooperate with the FBI in prosecuting mob boss John Gotti and other members of the Gambino family. An initial meeting was arranged between Gravano and an Iowa-born FBI agent named Bruce Moaw. As told in *Underboss*, a book by Peter Maas, the meeting began in the following way:

"Bruce Moaw walks over and shakes my hand [Gravano recalled]. He opened the door and I got in. I told him, 'Are you Moaw?' He says, 'Yes,' and I said, 'I heard you were from Iowa.'

He said that was right and I said, 'Well, if I got to trust somebody, it might as well be somebody from Iowa.' And off they went. " ■

Philippe Halsman, *Dali Atomicus* (1948), a detail from a photograph of Salvador Dali, airborne with water, cats, chair and easel. Public domain.

SALVADOR DALI
IN CEDAR FALLS

ANON

–How many surrealists does it take to screw in a lightbulb?
–Two: One to hold the giraffe and the other to fill the bathtub with brightly colored machine tools.

WHEN THE Spanish artist Salvador Dali was asked to name his favorite animal he answered, "filet of sole." He also said "I am surrealism" and defined it as "the systemization of confusion."

Dali was equally talented at self-promotion and money-making as he was at painting. As the French poet André Breton said: An anagram for Dali's name is *Avida Dollars*, a hybrid Spanish-English term for "eager for dollars."

Surrealism, which was founded by Breton in 1922, was a style of visual art and literature that resulted from an unlikely pairing of art with Freudian psychoanalysis.

Its artistic parent was a Zurich-based "anti-art" movement called Dada. Dada had begun as a protest of World War I and deliberately tried to antagonize its audiences through chance, nonsense, errors and contradiction—or, in other words, by the systemization of confusion.

IT WAS during that same war that Sigmund Freud's technique of "free association" (to say aloud while reclining on a couch whatever comes to mind) had been used with limited success in treating the victims of trench warfare.

Working with shell-shocked soldiers in a hospital, it was Breton who saw the connection between Freud's famous "talking cure" and the Dadaists' nonsense-producing game-like ploys of the *exquisite corpse, automatic writing*, and *radical juxtaposition*.

But the link between Freud and Breton was direct, and they actually met in Vienna in 1921. It is not as widely reported that Dali also met Freud, in 1938, in a meeting in London that, according to Dali, was an utter disappointment.

Freud was old and ill by then. Only a month earlier, he had withstood a Nazi raid of his home in Vienna, had fled to England, and would soon die of cancer of the jaw.

Given the circumstances, he could not have been greatly amused by a crank with billiard ball eyes and a moustache as sharp as a scorpion's tail.

"CONTRARY TO my hopes," Dali recalled of their meeting that day, "we spoke little, but we devoured each other with our eyes."

Dali, who was then in his mid-30's, was already becoming known for his "critical paranoid" paintings of dreams in which limp watches hang from trees, giraffes have been set afire, and Mae West is a cushioned room interior.

During his visit, Dali tried to convince Freud to look at an article that he had just published on paranoia. Opening its pages, he urged Freud to read it not as a "surrealist diversion" but as an "ambitiously scientific article." And yet, as Dali later reported, "Freud continued to stare at me without paying the slightest attention to my magazine."

Faced with what Dali described as such "imperturbable indifference," his voice grew "sharper and more insistent." After the meeting had ended, Dali added, Freud continued to look at him "with a fixity in which his whole being seemed to converge," then turned and said, in Dali's presence, to Stefan Zweig, the Austrian writer who had arranged the meeting, "I have never seen a more complete example of a Spaniard. *What a fanatic!*"

How wonderfully appropriate (how utterly dreamlike!) that the painter of dreams should prove incompatible with the father of dream analysis. No less appropriate, however, is the discovery that Dali's interpretation of Freud's reaction was mistaken, and that Freud actually found their encounter that afternoon both pleasant and instructive.

In other words, Dali really was paranoid. "I really owe you thanks for bringing yesterday's visitor... ," Freud wrote to Zweig on the day after the meeting. "For until now I have been inclined to regard the surrealists, who apparently have adopted me as their patron saint, as complete fools...That young Spaniard [Dali] with his candid, fantastical eyes, and his undeniable technical mastery, has changed my estimate."

IF ANY ENCOUNTER is more bizarre, or any juxtaposition more radical, a viable candidate may be the circumstances of fourteen years later, when Dali was briefly a visitor at the University of Northern Iowa (then called Iowa State Teachers College) in Cedar Falls.

Two years after his meeting with Freud, Dali had moved to the US, where he lived and worked for sixteen years, mostly in New York. Near the end of that period, having abandoned his critical paranoid stance and having been renounced by his fellow surrealists for his political beliefs, he agreed to a series of lectures in which he toured the country with his wife Gala, giving slide and chalkboard talks about his new approach to art called "nuclear mysticism."

In 1952, Dali gave ten such presentations at schools and museums throughout the US, beginning with a lecture on "Revolution and Tradition in Modern Painting" at UNI on the evening of Wednesday, February 6. His visit had been arranged by Herbert V. Hake, chairman of the college's Lecture Concert Series Committee, who had chosen Dali as a replacement for Edward R. Murrow, the celebrated CBS news analyst who was unable to appear.

Dali was paid a then-substantial speaking fee of $1,000. The only more expensive act was the Salzburg Marionettes.

Dali, Gala and Mr. and Mrs. A. Reynolds Morse (a couple from Cleveland, Ohio, who owned sixteen Dali paintings, and who later established the Salvador Dali Museum in St. Petersburg, Florida) arrived from Chicago by passenger train on the evening of February 5. They were housed in downtown Waterloo at the Russell Lamson Hotel where it had been agreed that at 10 o'clock the next morning Dali would hold a press conference.

ON WEDNESDAY evening, more than 1,300 people gathered for Dali's lecture, which began at 8 pm in the Auditorium of what is now Lang Hall. It was a huge audience for a small school, but dozens more might have attended, wrote *Des Moines Register* art critic George Shane, had it not taken place at the same time as an exhibition match by five Japanese Olympic wrestlers in the men's gymnasium across campus.

During his slide-illustrated lecture, Dali foretold the emergence of a new traditionalism, which he was the leading practitioner of, wherein artists would abandon the then popular Abstract Expressionism—which Dali characterized as "If you believe nothing, you can paint nothing"—and return to traditional narrative art, to "spiritual classicism."

It would be a second Renaissance, Dali predicted, in which academic painting practices (at which he excelled) would close the gap between science and religion, between rationality and mysticism.

"In spite of a tremendous language barrier," reported the student newspaper, Dali's audience of faculty, students and townspeople was both "charmed and fascinated" by his presentation.

"A Spaniard by birth," the article concluded, "Dali speaks English with a labored accent, seasoned with frequent French connectives and pronunciations. His colorful gestures, highly waxed moustache, distinctive cane, and ready wit added to his personal appeal."

In the audience that evening was Lester Longman, head of the School of Art and Art History at the University of Iowa in Iowa City. When the talk ended, he asked Dali about the political leanings of another Spaniard, Pablo Picasso. Were Picasso's paintings Communist?, asked Longman. No, replied Dali, they cannot even be exhibited in Russia.

Others wondered why an artist as famous as Dali had agreed to visit Iowa in the middle of winter. The answer, as it turned out, was that he had no grasp of the vastness of America. Looking at the map, Dali assumed that Cedar Falls, Kansas City, Houston and his other scheduled stops were only a brief train ride from Chicago.

Also in the audience was the painter Paul R. Smith, a University of Iowa graduate who had recently joined the UNI art faculty. In advance of the lecture, Smith had deliberately, cleverly placed blank sheets of brown kraft paper on the lectern and speaker's table in the hope that Dali might doodle or sketch inadvertently during the presentation.

Unfortunately, much later that evening, long after the lecture, when Smith went back to the Auditorium to retrieve the notes, scratches and drawings, they had been disposed of by the maintenance crew and lost.

THAT SAME evening, Smith and other UNI art faculty members, along with Longman and Shane, attended a party for Dali, which had been arranged by Harry G. Guillaume, the head of the art department.

Hosted by Corley Conlon, a legendary senior member of the art faculty, the party was held at her unconventional, self-designed cherry red home on Seerley Boulevard just west of the corner of Seerley and Main. On the basement level, there were no interior doors, so that Conlon could host parties at which everyone wore roller skates.

Throughout the party that evening, Smith remembered, "Dali and Longman spent most of the time talking in French.

Author's photograph of the former home of UNI faculty member Corley Conlon, on Seerley Boulevard in Cedar Falls, where the party for Salvador Dali took place in 1952. It is now an annex for artists studios at the Hearst Center for the Arts.

Dali, of course, would start an English sentence and then end two-thirds of it in French."

Dali said he liked the American Midwest because it reminded him of his own homeland. The corn in Iowa, he explained, "is the same as we have, except that ours is the red variety. We call it Arabian wheat, and the houses in Catalonia are beautiful when the ears are hung over the second floor balconies to dry."

IT WAS NOT Dali's thick accent but his distinctive rhinoceros hide cane, "which he used as sort of a riding crop and pointer," that left the most lasting impression that day on Donald A. Kelly—and for good reason.

At the time, Kelly worked in the school's Public Relations Office. He was not at the party at Conlon's house, but he was among the journalists and others who were present at the press conference in Waterloo earlier, on Wednesday morning.

During the question-and-answer period, Kelly asked Dali "if art critics might think his shift from Surrealism to nuclear mysticism could be a publicity ploy rather than genuine." The artist's alarming and sudden response was unforgettable: "He glared at me," recalled Kelly, "and slammed his cane on the table. If he responded verbally, I don't remember what he said."

Moments later, the news conference ended abruptly as the ex-Surrealist painter gave an especially fitting example of the systemization of confusion.

Wide-eyed, chin up, and fine-tuning the barbs of his moustache, he said: "Myself disagrees *avec* everybody today."

What a fanatic! ■

STEPHEN POTTER *One-Upmanship*
If your man says of some picture "Yes, but what does it mean?" ask him, and keep on asking him, what his carpet means, or the circular patterns on his rubber shoe soles. Make him lift up his foot and look at them.

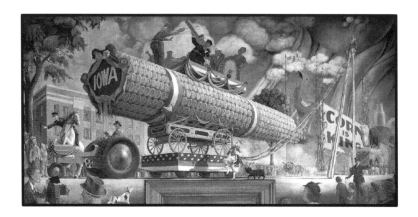

Author's photograph of Orr Cleveland Fisher's WPA mural (top), *The Corn Parade* (1941), as installed in the lobby of the US Post Office in Mount Ayr, Iowa. Below that is a snapshot of Fisher on a painting and camping trip in the 1920s, with his 1917 Maxwell Touring Car.

RINGGOLD COUNTY'S CORN PARADE

PEGGY WHITSON
...I figure if a farmer's daughter from Iowa can become an astronaut, you can be just about anything you want to be.

AMERICAN ASTRONAUT Peggy Whitson was born in south central Iowa, in Ringgold County, and attended high school in Mount Ayr, the county seat. She is that community's claim to fame, although it should also be noted that the parents of Jackson Pollock, the Abstract Expressionist artist, grew up in that county as well.

My favorite feather in the cap of Ringgold County is a Depression-era WPA mural that hangs in the US Post Office in Mount Ayr. Created in 1941 by local artist Orr Cleveland Fisher, it is titled *The Corn Parade*. I have admired it for years, but until recently, I had only seen reproductions.

A few years ago, I drove down to Mount Ayr, walked into the post office, and was delighted to see the mural first hand in all its glory. It is installed in the lobby, above the postmaster's office door. I photographed it from a low angle, without a ladder, which of course distorted the overall shape. But I was able to straighten it later and to restore its true proportion, using appropriate software.

OLDER READERS will already know about the WPA. It dates from the 1930s, during the Great Depression, when US President

Franklin D. Roosevelt created government subsidy programs to stabilize the economy by hiring the unemployed to work on public projects. The acronym WPA stood for the Works Progress Administration, an agency that oversaw the Public Works of Art Project (PWAP), the Federal Theatre Project (FTP), the Federal Writers Project (FWP), and other arts-based programs.

In Iowa, the PWAP regional director was Grant Wood. It was he who approved the artists who were commissioned by the government (at a salary of $26.50 to $42.50 per week) to create public murals, mostly for post office lobbies.

As many as thirty-five were commissioned for Iowa buildings, including two by Orr Fisher (in Mount Ayr and Forest City). The majority of those in Iowa have survived, although in some cases they have been relocated to libraries or city halls. Fisher completed his Mount Ayr mural nearly eighty years ago, and Ringgold County is fortunate that it still hangs on the wall it was made for. If you haven't seen it, you really should make the pilgrimage.

THE CORN PARADE is utterly charming and funny. It is a colorful, cartoon-style daydream of a harvest parade in an Iowa farming community. Its central feature is a float being towed by a tractor. Walking alongside are a trained pig and a marching clown, followed by an unbelievably tall Uncle Sam on stilts.

On a wagon on the float is a gigantic ear of corn, too large for any wagon, like those huge Paul Bunyan vegetables on humorous antique postcards. On top of the corn is a box-like platform for three musicians, who are following the raised baton of an eccentric-looking band leader. An ear of corn as massive as this must surely have resulted from a record-breaking corn harvest.

Now that is something to crow about, a rooster on the corn

proclaims, and a billboard on the right contends that CORN IS KING.

When asked about the mural, Fisher replied that some of its characters were based on actual residents of Ringgold County. For example, one of the figures is the Mount Ayr postmaster, above whose door the mural would hang. The mayor of the city is mounted on a horse on the left, and the photographer, tractor driver, and others were also local citizens.

ORR FISHER'S *The Corn Parade* is not an easel painting, but a large wall mural that measures 11 feet wide and 5 feet high. Fisher had twice studied briefly with the French Academy-trained Iowa artist Charles A. Cumming at his Cumming School of Art in Des Moines.

Other than that, Fisher was self-taught, or learned through correspondence schools. He recalled that from an early age, he was preoccupied with drawing, an interest that never abated. As he put it, "everywhere I have gone I have drawn. I have drawn almost everything imaginable…except a salary."

He had an inexhaustible interest in illustration, design and cartooning, and he especially admired the drawings of Ding Darling, the celebrated *Des Moines Register* editorial cartoonist, who was also a conservationist.

In every square inch, there is a whimsical energy in *The Corn Parade*. As restless as a rolling stone, the zany mural reflects the zigzag paths in Fisher's life. After flunking Latin and German at Drake University in his early twenties, he "quit school and went West."

IN WYOMING, as he later recalled, he "got work on a ranch …organized a Sunday School; drove an eight-horse freight team with one line 90 miles across the desert; slept on the ground and in a covered wagon when 40 degrees below zero; heard the coyotes howl; rode a four-horse load of pine logs down the mountain behind a run-away team, but escaped with only bruises; fell through the ice riding a horse across a mountain stream, jumped to solid ice and escaped, but the horse chilled to death; bet Uncle Sam that I could live on a quarter section of land, and I won the bet; built a log cabin, hunted deer and elk and really ate bear meat."

HE WAS ALSO an erstwhile inventor, and, at age 19, he was granted a US Patent (No. 759,257) for an *Automatic Whistle Operating Mechanism* for locomotives.

Later, having returned to Iowa from his adventures in the West, he worked as an electrical signalman for the railroad, made illustrations and cartoons for signalman publications, and worked as an advertising artist for a farm implement company in Waterloo, Iowa. But after while, he gave that up and, once again, he headed West.

For a while, he toured scenic vistas in "Max" (a 1917 Maxwell Touring Car in which he camped), painting landscapes *en plein air*. He made comical "get well soon" greeting cards that were sold in hospital gift shops.

He also spent some time out East, where he built a studio and joined the artists' colony at Woodstock, New York. In the last phase of his life, he went West a final time, settled in California, and died in 1974 in Fresno.

In retrospect, Orr Fisher led his life as a kind of parade. He was a free spirit, always in motion—and always marching to a drum that only he himself could hear. ∎

SURVIVING WPA MURALS IN IOWA

City   Artist   Location Site   Date Completed

Algona Francis Robert White / Public Library / 1941
Ames Lowell Houser / Post Office / 1938
Audubon Virginia Snedeker / Post Office / 1942
Bloomfield John Sharp / Post Office / 1940
Cedar Rapids Francis Robert White / Courthouse / 1937
Clarion Paul Faulkner / Post Office / 1943
Columbus Junction Sante Graziani / Post Office / 1942
Corning Marion Gilmore / Post Office / 1941
Corydon Marion Gilmore / Post Office / 1942
Cresco Richard Haines / Post Office / 1937
De Witt John Bloom / City Hall / 1938
Dubuque Bertrand R. Adams / Post Office / 1937
Dubuque William Bunn / Post Office / 1937
Emmetsburg Lee Allen / Post Office / 1940
Forest City Orr Fisher / Post Office / 1942
Hamburg William Bunn / Post Office / 1941
Harlan Richard Gates / Post Office / 1937
Hawarden John Sharp / Post Office / 1942
Ida Grove Andreen Kauffman / Post Office / 1940
Independence Robert Tabor / Post Office / 1938
Jefferson Tom Savage / Post Office / 1938
Knoxville Marvin Beerbohn / Post Office / 1941
Leon A. Chris Glasell / Post Office / 1938
Manchester William Henning / Post Office / 1938
Marion Daniel Rhodes / City Hall / 1939
Missouri Valley Francis Robert White / Post Office / 1938
Monticello William Palmer / Post Office / 1941
Mount Ayr Orr Fisher / Post Office / 1941
Mount Pleasant Dorothea Tomlinson / Post Office / 1939
New Hampton Tom Savage / Post Office / 1939
Onowa Lee Allen / Post Office / 1938
Osceola Byron Boyd / Post Office / 1936
Pella Byron Boyd / Post Office / 1938
Rockwell City John Sharp / Post Office / 1941
Sigourney Richard Olsen / Post Office / 1940
Storm Lake Daniel Rhodes / Public Library / 1937
Tipton John Bloom / Post Office / 1940
Waterloo Edgar Britton / Public Library / 1940
Waverly Mildred Pelzer Lynch / Post Office / 1938

Fort Atkinson barracks, c1919

Author's montage from public domain components

HOLDING DOWN
THE FORT'S REMAINS

JOHN W. GARDNER *No Easy Victories*
History never looks like history when you are living through it. It always looks confusing and messy, and it always feels uncomfortable.

IN 1920, an Iowa writer named Woodworth Clum published a volume titled *Making Socialists Out of College Students: A Story of Professors and Other Collegians Who Hobnob with Radicals,* in which he voiced concerns about "pink professors" and the threat of "college bolshevism."

Clum's father was a newspaper publisher named John P. Clum, who had been a "Western hero" of sorts. In the 1870s, as the Indian agent at the San Carlos Reservation in Arizona, he achieved acclaim when he captured Geronimo without firing a shot.

He went on to become the first mayor of Tombstone, founded *The Epitaph* newspaper there, and was unremitting in his defense of controversial lawman Wyatt Earp. In 1936, the younger Clum produced a book about his father's life, titled *Apache Agent.* It later became a Hollywood film, called *Walking the Proud Land* (1956), with Audie Murphy playing the role of the elder Clum.

BY 1919, Woodworth Clum had become the director of The Greater Iowa Association, and, as part of that position, he was touring regions of the state. Given his father's background as well as his own interest in the history of the relations between

Native Americans and Euro-American immigrants, he drove south from Decorah, with the intention of exploring a bygone American Army post called Fort Atkinson. It must have been easy to locate, since a small adjacent town had been given the same name.

Constructed in 1841, the historic fort's buildings consisted of a barracks for enlisted men, an officers' quarters, two block houses (with gun and cannon ports), a powder house, a supply warehouse, and a chapel.

Made of stone walls two feet thick, these buildings lined the perimeter of a parade ground and were additionally shielded by wood-log stockade walls, from the top of which the soldiers could view the Turkey River, which flows through the scenic valley below.

It is commonly claimed that Fort Atkinson was the only US Army fort that was built for the primary purpose of protecting one Native American group (the Winnebago or Ho-Chunk) from aggressive encroachments by others (including whites), by monitoring a neutral zone.

But five years after the fort was built, its soldiers were reassigned to fight in the Mexican War. It was briefly maintained by Iowa troops, but when the Winnebago were relocated in 1849, it no longer had a reason to be. Four years later, the land and its buildings were auctioned off to the public for three and a half thousand dollars.

IN 1919, WHEN Woodworth Clum drove up the hill from the town of Fort Atkinson in search of that historic fort, he was disheartened by what he found. "At the top of the hill," he remembered, "we turned to the left and came alongside an old stone building, half crumbled away." This was the remains of the barracks.

Half of the barracks had all but collapsed, but the remaining half was lived in by what Clum decribed as "a farmer's family." "I asked the wife," he later wrote, "as she stood over the washtub in the yard, to tell me where I could find old Fort Atkinson." She answered that this was all that was left.

As he walked the property with his camera, he found that one of the buildings was shelter for the family's pigs. The place was a literal "pigsty," he wrote. A cow grazed in the central square. The storehouse was used as a hen house, and chickens were running around in the ruins of the powder magazine.

Clum was more than just dismayed that day—he was distraught. Weeks later, he published an article in the September issue of *Iowa Magazine* with the provocative title "Fort Atkinson, A Pigsty."

"Oh, Iowa!" his article pleaded: Have material needs gotten the better of us? Have we not gone overboard in sacrificing our history in favor of pork, eggs, milk, and rental fees? "Who is the man—or woman—of the hour who will lead a campaign to have old Fort Atkinson restored: to have a good road built to it, and make of it what it should be—a mecca for those who love Iowa, and her history?"

I LEARNED ABOUT Woodworth Clum only recently. He died the year that I was born. On the day he toured the ruins of Fort Atkinson, he could not have known that the farmer's wife to whom he spoke was my grandmother, Christina Wilhelmina Marie Brandt Behrens.

She was my father's mother, and my father (who was then eighteen) may or may not have been present that day. Clum took photographs during his visit, and, in a view of the barracks, there is a young man at the top of the stairs, who may have been my father or his look-alike brother George. Other children can be seen, not clearly enough to recognize, in other photographs by Clum.

When he spoke to the wife of "the farmer" that day, Clum was apparently oblivious of the whereabouts of the farmer. That farmer *in absentia* was my paternal grandfather, Diedrich Joseph Gottlieb Behrens.

He could not be present because in August of the previous year, while harvesting crops with his neighbors, his clothing became caught up in the moving parts of a threshing machine. I can't describe the death he endured, because I don't entirely know the facts—but also because it horrifies me to even begin to imagine the scene.

Needless to say, he was pronounced dead when the doctor arrived.

The author's aunt and two uncles (his father's siblings) standing behind their father's tombstone. Collection of Richard H. Behrens.

IN MY BROTHER'S family research files, there is a sorrowful photograph of our grandmother as a young widow, a few days after our grandfather's death. She is standing behind the youngest three of the couple's seven children. Beside them in the photograph is Aunt Helena, my grandfather's sister, who had come to console her sister-in-law, as well as to softly propose to "adopt" one or more of the youngest children.

But my grandmother insisted on keeping them all, even though, as a result of recent crop failures, she and the children were destined to be penniless. Unable to stay on the farm they leased, they were soon without a place to live.

In the days that followed my grandfather's death—again, I don't know the full details—my grandmother was able to live temporarily in the ruins of the fort, which was privately owned at the time.

They apparently lived there for most of a year, more or less, because they were no doubt the family (with the widow outdoors at the washtub) that was belittled in Clum's appeal to restore a landmark from Iowa's past.

All's well that ends well. Or so we say.

My grandmother and her children (my father, aunts and uncles) were eventually able to move to a more conventional home in the small adjoining town of Fort Atkinson. Clum's preservation campaign was launched, and the historic fort was reacquired by the State of Iowa in 1921.

Its formal restoration began in 1958, and it was given the status of a State Preserve. Today it is all but resplendent, and the popular site of a festival for reenactments of pioneer life. ■

CAPTAIN BASIL HALL *Travels in North America*
The resemblance to the sea which some of the prairies exhibited was really most singular. I had heard of this before, but always supposed the account exaggerated…the distant insulated trees, as they gradually rose above the horizon, or receded from our view…were so exactly like strange sails heaving in sight, that I am sure, if two or three sailors had been present, they would almost have agreed as to what canvas these magical vessels were carrying.

WILLIAM JAMES AND JOSIAH ROYCE

Author's montage from public domain components

A TURBID AND UNFRIENDLY TREK

ANON

The phrase "selling shovels in a gold rush" originated after the California Gold Rush, when it became clear that most prospectors didn't make any money but the suppliers who sold them shovels did.

IN THE SPRING of 1891, a 72-year-old woman was dropping off a letter at the post office in San Jose, California, when a man—who was exceptionally large, unsteady, and walking at a frantic pace—suddenly collided with her.

His head struck hers so forcefully that she fell against a nearby wall, leaving a gash on her forehead. She regained her balance and appeared to recover in a few moments. But several days later, she began to experience swelling, bleeding, weakness, loss of appetite, shortness of breath, and other effects.

IN THE MONTHS that followed, her health continued to weaken, and she died at home of "nervous shock" on the evening of Tuesday, November 24, 1891, attended by her daughter. Her married name was Sarah Royce, while her parents' family name was Bayliss.

Originally from England, she had been born in 1819 in Stratford-upon-Avon, William Shakespeare's birthplace. When she was only six weeks old, her family immigrated to America and settled in Rochester, New York.

The Bayliss family was reasonably well-off, and Sarah was fortunate to be among the few women at the time who were able to become well-educated, even to go on to college. She became Sarah Royce in May of 1845, when she married a slightly older man, who was also British-born.

They remained in Rochester for three years, but then decided to set out for more sparsely settled Western land. That land of course had long been claimed by Native Americans, whose concepts of "land ownership" and "settlement" were more than a little at odds with the traditions of the newly arrived Euro-Americans.

BY EARLY 1849, Sarah Royce and her husband Josiah were living in a small community about three miles from Tipton, Iowa, 60 miles west of the Mississippi River.

There had been a flurry of rumors about the abundance of unclaimed land in California. They had also heard that gold was found, the year before, at Sutter's Creek, about 45 miles east of Sacramento.

They soon joined the ranks of those who were called the "Forty-Niners" because, in 1849, they packed their essential belongings in covered wagons, and all but blindly headed west.

The Royces left Iowa on the last day of April that year. They traveled with other wagons as a rule. But it was difficult to keep up, in part because Sarah was unwaveringly religious, a strict adherent of the Disciples of Christ. As a result, she insisted on resting on the Sabbath, with the result that she and her husband (with a two-year-old daughter) sometimes lost sight of the wagons ahead.

THE IMMENSITY of their journey, powered by three yokes of oxen, from Iowa to California, soon became apparent. It took them an entire day to reach the town of Tipton, having traveled only three miles.

It then required another week (including inert Sundays) to reach Iowa City, from where they headed further west. While passing through Fort Des Moines, they were warned of an outbreak of cholera in Council Bluffs, but they pressed on regardless.

Covered wagons that are more or less comparable to those that the Royce family traveled in. Public domain. Wikimedia Commons.

Arriving at Council Bluffs by early June, they found a "city of wagons," all of which were waiting in line to be ferried across the "turbid and unfriendly" Missouri River.

It was there that they also encountered Native Americans, whom Sarah described in her journal as "begging and pilfering Indians." She continued: "You could not give them anything–giving a thing to one would bring a dozen more to you. You had to keep them at a distance–not be friendly."

They would have later encounters with such "hostiles," but it was far more apparent that the real threats to their lives would come not from Indians, but from the ailments that they were transporting in their bodies: scarlet fever, cholera, small pox, measles, tuberculosis, diphtheria, mumps, and other contagious diseases.

IT WAS LATE in the travel season, and the Royces were among the last to cross the Missouri River. They would need to travel doggedly in order to pass through the mountains before the winter snows began. Still, Sarah insisted on resting on Sundays, while the other wagons moved ahead.

They succeeded in crossing the Rockies, and soon after reached the Great Salt Lake. But hazardous travel loomed ahead: Fresh water was scarce, and the desert heat was so intense that they rested in the shade during daylight, and traveled in the dark of night.

The pace of the near-starving oxen (some of which perished) was so ponderous that Sarah walked alone ahead. In the darkness, she and the rest of her party failed to see a turn-off for a short cut that would ensure their survival.

At last, in desperation, having seen roadside evidence of victims of the same mistake, they turned back and retraced their steps. They succeeded in crossing the desert, the Carson River, and the Sierra Nevada mountains with the help of government scouts. At last, they reached Weaverville, in northern California (about 100 miles east of Eureka) in October 1849.

HOW DO WE know all this? I confess that I myself did not, until recently. But then I remembered a book by F.O. Matthiessen that I had read many years ago. Titled *The James Family*, it is a wonderfully rich account of the various interactions among the brothers William and Henry James, along with their parents and siblings.

William James is among my favorite philosophers, and on page 422 of that book is an unforgettable pair of photographs.

They show in sequence two snapshots of James, seated on an old stone wall at his summer farm in the White Mountains, near Chocorua, New Hampshire.

William James (left) and Josiah Royce at James' country home in 1903. Public domain. Wikimedia Commons.

Conversing, while seated beside him, is his amiable, younger friend, a philosophy colleague at Harvard, named Josiah Royce. As the camera clicked, the ever-joking James exclaimed, "Royce, you're being photographed! Look out! I say Damn the Absolute!"

THAT HARVARD professor, Josiah Royce, was the son of Sarah (Bayliss) Royce, who walked from Tipton, Iowa, to Weaverville, California. His father was Josiah Royce, Sr., of course.

The younger Royce was born in 1855, and grew up in California. At some point, it was that same admiring son who persuaded his aging mother to share her candid diaries from that astonishing journey. Readily available now, they were published in 1932 as *A Frontier Lady: Recollections of the Gold Rush and Early California* (Yale University Press). ■

Portrait photograph of Buffalo Bill Cody (c1892). Public domain. Wikimedia.

THE RIOTOUS
WILD WEST

BUFFALO BILL
My debut upon the world's stage occurred on
February 26, 1846, in the State of Iowa.

WORLD WAR ONE began in Europe in the fall of 1914. But the US remained neutral until April 1917, when it declared war on Germany, partly because of the sinking of the RMS *Lusitania*, a British passenger liner. Included among the fatalities were 128 Americans, and the motto of those who demanded revenge was "Remember the *Lusitania*."

Iowa-born Wild West showman William Frederick Cody, known as Buffalo Bill, was fortunate not to have witnessed the final years of the Great War. He died on January 10, 1917, in Denver, Colorado, at age 70.

His funeral was a major news event, as admirers worldwide mourned his passing. Ironically, despite the on-going conflict, condolences for his death were sent by both England's King George V and Germany's Kaiser Wilhelm II.

CODY'S DEATH was undoubtedly fresh in American minds on March 6, 1917, less than two months after the funeral. On that day, according to an article in the *Marshalltown* (Iowa) *Times-Republican*, a group of Iowa youngsters, who were walking down the street in Cedar Falls, had the strangest encounter in their lives. For a moment, they saw walking toward them a living, breathing Buffalo Bill.

FIVE YEARS EARLIER, on August 31, 1912, Buffalo Bill's Wild West extravaganza had performed in Cedar Falls. His crew had set up their arena on the city's northwest corner, in Mullarkey's Pasture (near what is now called Riverview Park).

Now, in 1917, the youngsters were sure it was Buffalo Bill who was walking toward them on the street. As described by the Marshalltown news story, this man—he was the same height as Buffalo Bill—had Cody's "flowing hair, moustache, goatee, big sombrero, and cowboy boots," even his famous baby-blue eyes. What a shock!

"Look, fellers," cried out one of the youngsters, "Buffalo Bill ain't dead!"

In the end, it was all an innocent error—of sorts. The man walking toward them was indeed a "dead ringer" for Cody, but he was not the genuine Buffalo Bill.

He was instead a performer and a long-time friend of the showman, a man named Curt L. Alexander from Hastings, Nebraska. Originally from Leon, Iowa (at the bottom center of the state), he was traveling by train back to Hastings from Chicago, and decided to stop over in Cedar Falls to visit his Iowa nephew, a downtown clothing merchant named Lloyd Alexander.

THE YOUNGSTERS could hardly be faulted. They were certainly not the first to mistake Curt Alexander for Bill Cody. Earlier news stories had reported on a trip that Alexander had made to the East Coast about ten years before. There, "he was greeted everywhere as Buffalo Bill and in Boston the newspaper men refused to believe his denial."

The same thing happened in St Joseph, Missouri. As noted in the *Nebraska State Journal* in 1909, "Mr. Alexander bears a strong resemblance to Colonel Cody and has often been mistaken for him by intimate friends of Mr. Cody."

At times, it may have been purposeful for Alexander to be mistaken for Buffalo Bill, because he was then able (as were several others) to step in as Cody's double. As the hero aged, there were rumors that he had found it an increasing challenge to mount his horse, much less to ride around waving his hat.

Photograph of Sitting Bull and Buffalo Bill, Montreal (1885). William Notman and Son. Public domain. Wikimedia.

AS WAS STANDARD for the Wild West's traveling agenda, Cody appeared in a number of Iowa towns in 1912, including

Muscatine (July 24), Iowa City (July 25), Oelwein (July 26), Decorah (July 27), Charles City (July 29), Dubuque (August 29), Manchester (August 30), Cedar Falls (August 31), Iowa Falls (September 2), Webster City (September 3), Cherokee (September 4), Sheldon (September 5), and Sioux City (September 7). My father attended the show in Decorah that year, when he was eleven years old.

Back to Cedar Falls on August 31, a resident named Stella Wynegar did not attend the performance, but her son Claud did. Later that day, she drove out to the grounds in a buggy to pick up her son. She recalled that as they "were wandering around…Buffalo Bill came up and talked with us. He asked about our family and told us about his life and where he'd been. He was very interesting and nice."

That same day presumably, another Cedar Falls resident, a girl whose family lived on West First Street (near the performance location) was sitting outside when Buffalo Bill "came walking along and saw the chickens in our yard. He offered my grandma $1.50 [equal to $40 today] to cook a chicken dinner for his troupe and she did it!"

TO BE TRUTHFUL, not all the midwestern engagements of the Wild West were free of controversy. The most egregious example occurred in Prairie du Chien, Wisconsin, on the night of August 20, 1900.

At the end of two hot summer shows, a number of Cody's performers gathered to drink and play cards at a bar. They started a tab, but the bartender grew impatient when they seemed indifferent to paying the bill. When he threatened them with a pistol, they grabbed the gun and attacked him.

The ruckus attracted attention, and a local armed policeman arrived and threatened to detain everyone. In response, the cowboys went after the lawman, who fled down the street then suddenly turned and fired a shot that struck a cowboy in the arm.

With that, a veritable riot ensued, with Cody's cowboys up against angry townspeople. As violence and property damage increased, someone sent a telegram to the governor of Wisconsin, who wired Cody in return, threatening to send in the National Guard.

Unaware of all the commotion, Buffalo Bill had retired for the night. After reading the governor's wire, he strapped on two loaded pistols, and shouted angrily "Get my horse!" Arriving in town, he used a whistle to summon his men, and ordered them to fall into formation.

And then, as if nothing had happened, he marched them silently back to the grounds. The riot having ended, the threat of the National Guard was withdrawn. By daybreak the following morning, the Wild West troupe had disappeared—it had quietly moved on to the next town on its schedule. ■

KATE E. GLASPELL *Annie Oakley and Buffalo Bill's Wild West*
When Sitting Bull was called upon [to speak to an audience of businessmen] the soldier [serving as his translator] motioned to him and he rose clumsily, but to the astonishment and horror of the soldier, said: "I hate you. I hate you. I hate all the white people. You are thieves and liars. You have taken away our land and made us outcasts, so I hate you." The soldier, sure there were very few in the audience with any knowledge of the [Sioux] language, realized it was up to him to preserve peace. He sat quietly until Sitting Bull had finished and then, probably with every hair on his head standing on end, he rose smiling and delivered, as the interpretation, the friendly, courteous speech he had prepared which met with approval of the crowd.

Gertrude Käsebier (1903), portrait photograph of Evelyn Nesbit. Public domain.
Wikimedia Commons.

HOT FRANKFURTERS
ON UNBUTTERED BREAD

DOROTHEA LANGE
**A camera is an instrument that teaches
people how to see without a camera.**

ON THE EVENING of June 25, 1906, during a performance at Madison Square Garden in New York, a millionaire named Harry Thaw drew a pistol. Standing two feet behind a prominent architect and socialite named Stanford White, he fired three times into his back, killing White instantly.

Thaw had recently married a chorus girl and actress named Evelyn Nesbit. In an effort to be straightforward, she revealed to him that, several years earlier, as a teenager, she had been sedated and seduced by White.

At the time of the shooting, the public was well-acquainted with Nesbit. She was a highly popular model for artists and photographers, and a "Gibson girl" celebrity.

THE BEST-KNOWN portrait of Nesbit, made in 1903, is an iconic image in the history of photography. The woman who made it, Iowa native Gertrude Käsebier (1852-1934), is now widely considered to be one of the finest photographers of the Modern era. That ranking is not only based on her portrait of Nesbit—indeed, she was far more accomplished than that.

Käsebier (née Gertrude Stanton) had a photographic studio on Fifth Avenue in New York at the time that she photographed Nesbit. Her photographic career had taken off late in the 1890s, when Alfred Stieglitz published and exhibited her photographs.

Kasebier was, said Stieglitz, "the leading artistic portrait photographer of the day." In 1903, six of her works were included in the first issue of his *Camera Work*, the celebrated journal of the Photo-Secessionist movement.

AS AN ADULT, Käsebier lived most of her life in the east, but her childhood was more diverse than that. She was born in 1852 in Des Moines, Iowa, and spent her first eight years in what was then called Fort Des Moines. When her family moved westward to profit from providing supplies to prospectors, her father became the first mayor of Golden, Colorado.

It was while living in Iowa and Colorado that she became intrigued by Native Americans, especially Lakota Sioux. She later recalled that, during her childhood, it was a simpler, less treacherous time.

The Indian women who lived nearby would ask her parents to borrow her, "take her to play with [their children], spend the day, and then send her back to her mother with her apron filled with buffalo meat." It was a time when buffalo were plentiful, and her indigenous neighbors were largely benign.

SOME FORTY YEARS later, those childhood memories came back to Käsebier as she looked out from the window of her New York studio to see the colorful grand parade of Buffalo Bill's Wild West.

Leading that procession on horseback was the illustrious William F. Cody, who was escorting his famous troupe toward Madison Square Garden, where they would perform for the next several weeks.

Käsebier was entranced, and soon after she drafted a letter to Cody, asking his permission to make photographic portraits of the Native Americans in his show. Cody granted her request, and she was then able to set up a studio session on Sunday, April 24, 1898.

Gertrude Käsebier (c1900), portrait photograph of Amos Two Bulls. Public domain. Wikimedia Commons.

That morning, nine Sioux men and their chaperone arrived at her studio (one hour early) for a serving of tea and "hot frankfurters on unbuttered bread." They were dressed in their finest traditional outfits, which they were permitted to wear by the government whenever they traveled with Cody. In contrast, when living on the reservation, they were expected to dress in "civilized" Euro-American clothes, for the purpose of learning to assimilate.

At the end of refreshments, Käsebier (described as "an old friend of their tribe") took photographs of her colorful guests for three hours. The group of nine included Chief Iron Tail, High Heron, Has-No-Horses, Samuel Lone Bear, Joseph Black Fox, Red Horn Bull, Shooting Pieces, Phillip Standing Soldier, and Kills-Close-to-the-Lodge. Twenty-two years had passed since the Battle of the Little Big Horn (in which Iron Tail may have participated), and a mere seven years had elapsed since the Seventh Cavalry's massacre of several hundred Lakota Sioux at Wounded Knee.

THE PORTRAITS Käsebier made that day (now accessible online at the Library of Congress Prints and Photographs website) are both candid and dignified, the inverse of standardized studio views. In the words of Michelle Delaney (author of *Buffalo Bill's Wild West Warriors: A Photographic History by Gertrude Käsebier*), Käsebier's photographs were "simple, thought-provoking, modern portraits of individuals involved in a cultural transition."

Gertrude Käsebier (c1900), portrait photographs of Charging Thunder (left) and Plenty Wounds. Public domain. Wikimedia Commons.

This was not an exploitive commercial affair. Käsebier's portraits were not used for Wild West advertising, nor were they sold as gallery art. That initial session led to a long-term alliance between the photographer and her new-found friends.

They soon had subsequent contacts, exchanges of letters and notes, and additional portrait sessions. She attended their performances whenever they were in New York, and, in turn, they gave her drawings they made during visits to her studio.

Before the first studio visit, someone cautioned Käsebier that if she invited them once, they would mistakenly consider it "the equivalent of a declaration of friendship for life." They

Gertrude Käsebier (c1900), group portrait of Wild West performers drawing in Käsebier's studio. Public domain. Wikimedia Commons.

would repeatedly visit her studio, invited or not.

To which Käsebier replied, "Let them come…" recalling her childhood on the plains, "I shall be glad to see them." ■

EVAN S. CONNELL *Son of the Morning Star*

Thomas Henry Tibbles…remarked that Indians, who never shake hands among themselves, consider this act to be one of the funniest things in the world. Nevertheless, having learned that whites express friendship by seizing each other, they happily do the same.

Napoleon Sarony (1882), portrait photograph of Oscar Wilde. Public domain.

WILDE, WHISKEY
AND THE PEACOCK ROOM

JOHN RUSKIN
**Remember that the most beautiful things in the world are
the most useless; peacocks and lilies for instance.**

IN THE LAST years of the 19th century, the Aesthetic Movement
was regarded by some as offensive. Famously tied to the slogan
"Art for Art's Sake," it was especially abhorrent to men, who
considered it a challenge to the virtues of brazen machismo.

Its male proponents—its Aesthetes—were mercilessly made
fun of, including such artists and writers as James A.M. Whistler,
Oscar Wilde, Algernon Charles Swinborne (nicknamed Swine-
born by critics), and Aubrey Beardsley (known as Awfully
Weirdly).

They and others were said to promote "unmanly manhood."
They were "preening peacocks," who, by "squandering virility for
beauty," were diluting the rough-and-ready of men.

In 1881, the British comic opera team Gilbert and Sullivan
joined the ranks of dissenters who delighted in lampooning
Aesthetes.

They wrote a comic opera (one of their most successful)
titled *Patience, or Bunthorne's Bride*. Central to the story are two
poetic characters named Reginald Bunthorne and Archibald
Grosvenor. Both wore Buster Brown costumes comprised of
items matching those of Wilde, Swinborne, and Whistler,
including Whistler's monocle. The production was a resounding
success, and continued for 578 performances.

THE POPULARITY of *Patience* in England prompted the idea of taking it on a traveling tour to North America. But for that to succeed, the American public would need to be better acquainted with the Aesthetic Movement, as well as its leading adherents.

As a result, Oscar Wilde, who was in need of income, agreed to serve as a *de facto* publicist, in which he would prepare the way for the opera by touring and talking about Aestheticism in the US and Canada. His tour, which was expected to last four months, began in New York in January of 1882. Sometimes well-received, sometimes not, his stay was extended for nearly a year.

Wilde spent the first six weeks traveling and giving talks about "The English Renaissance" on the East Coast, in New York State, and in parts of New England. Over a period of almost eleven months, he lectured 141 times, the last of which occurred in New York on November 27.

Twenty-one of his appearances took place in Canada, while the remaining 120 were given as he toured the rest of the US, including the Midwest, West, Southwest, South, and East. He was featured in programs in Iowa at Dubuque, Sioux City, Des Moines, Iowa City, Cedar Rapids, and the Quad Cities.

WHEN INTERVIEWED in Sioux City, he was described by a news reporter as "ladylike." The article continued: "He occasionally moistened his wrists in a preoccupied way with perfume from a tiny flat vial. His large, liquid eyes rolled upwards at times as he became interested, something as a schoolgirl's when she speaks to an intimate friend of her latest love affair."

Wilde himself recalled that his Sioux City audience was no less "interested and sympathetic" than others to whom he had spoken, while the newspaper described the audience as "common people, farmers, mechanics and others of a simple grade of life."

Cedar Rapids was considerably less polite. In anticipation of Wilde's arrival, the newspaper asked what the city had done "to be thus afflicted? We thought the scarlet fever was scourge enough for one season....Have your sunflower seeds planted and your statuary well covered with dust."

Yet, that was far more welcoming than the disingenuous invitation in the *Cincinnati Enquirer*: "If Mr. Oscar Wilde will leave his lilies and daffodils and come to Cincinnati, we will undertake to show him how to deprive thirty hogs of their intestines in one minute."

PERHAPS THE most fabled event on his tour was his appearance at the Tabor Opera House in Leadville, Colorado, on April 13, 1882, where he lectured on the subject of "The Decorative Arts."

Leadville was a gnarly mining town, and Wilde had been forewarned that he might be shot if he visited there. It had also been rumored "that an attempt would be made by a number of young men to ridicule him by coming to the lecture in exaggerated aesthetic costumes, with enormous sunflowers and lilies, and to introduce a number of hard characters in the traditional costume of the Western 'Bad Men.'"

But quite the opposite occurred. The miners lowered him down the shaft in a bucket to the bottom of the silver mine (he was no doubt on their "bucket list"), where they treated him to a sham banquet, the menu of which (as Wilde recalled) was as follows: "The first course was whiskey, the second course was whiskey and the third course was whiskey!"

Astonished that a namby-pamby Aesthete could imbibe as much as even a raucous miner, they invited him to use a ceremonial drill to open a new source of silver, which was then christened "Oscar." He was given the drill as a keepsake.

SO WHAT IS all this other stuff about peacocks, sunflowers, and lilies? Reporters often asked just that, because those items had been prominent in Gilbert and Sullivan's opera.

Wilde replied that, as an Aesthete, he was fond of sunflowers and lilies because, "of all our flowers in England, [they are] the

Photograph (top) of the original collection of Asian ceramics in the London home of Frederick Richards Leyland. Below that is the current Peacock Room, designed by James A.M. Whistler, as reconstructed at the Freer Gallery of Art at the Smithsonian Institution in Washington DC. Public domain.

most perfect models of design."

As for peacocks, when they unfurl their tail feathers, the patterns of the "eyespots" match the spiral patterns (based on the Fibonacci number sequence) in sunflowers, pinecones, and the rose-themed stained glass windows in Gothic cathedrals. Given all its mystical qualities, the peacock had long been a common motif in Chinese and Japanese arts and crafts.

SIX YEARS IN advance of Wilde's American tour, Whistler had been commissioned to design a room in the home of a wealthy British art collector, for the purpose of housing his plunder of Asian ceramics. Because Whistler chose to use a peacock as a repeated motif in that project, it is called *Harmony in Blue and Gold: The Peacock Room*.

The Peacock Room was purchased in 1904 by the American industrialist Charles Lang Freer. Dismantled, its components were brought to this country, and, in 1919, it was permanently reconstructed at the Freer Gallery of Art at the Smithsonian Institution in Washington DC, where it awaits your visit.

It is a monument to the Aesthetic Movement, to the wisdom of Whistler and Oscar Wilde—and proof of an Aesthete's acumen. ■

JAMES HILLMAN *Cosmos, Life, Religion*
Animal life is biologically esthetic: each species presents itself in design, coats, tails, feathers, furs, curls, tusks, horns, hues, sheens, shells, scales, wings, songs, dances.

SHAKER MAXIM
Every force evolves a form.

Josiah Johnson Hawes (1857), photographic portrait of Ralph Waldo Emerson. Public domain. Wikimedia Commons.

WHEN EMERSON
WALKED ON WATER

WALT WHITMAN
**He [Emerson] has what none else has; he does what none else
does....He represents the freeman, America, the individual.**

IN THE IOWA TOWN where I grew up, the city's public schools
were known as Washington, Emerson, Lincoln and Hawthorne.
Indeed, throughout the country, it was common for public
schools to be named in honor of these same individuals. I
attended Emerson School for five years, from kindergarten
through fourth grade, then spent two years at Washington for
the fifth and sixth grades.

Back then I knew little or nothing about the New England
poet and philosopher Ralph Waldo Emerson (1803-1882), who
was among the founders of Transcendentalism.

I was certainly unaware that he had toured the country in the
mid-19th century, giving talks in twenty states, including Iowa.
Indeed, few speakers were as popular, as shown by the fact that
Emerson gave fifteen hundred talks in more than three hundred
American towns.

ACCORDING TO a 1927 article by Iowa historian Hubert H.
Hoeltje, titled "Ralph Waldo Emerson in Iowa," Emerson first saw
Iowa in the summer of 1850, but only from a distance. He viewed
it from the eastern bank of the Mississippi River, near Galena. It
was not until five years later that he set foot on Iowa soil, by
which time it had been a state for nearly a decade.

In 1855, he was invited to lecture in Davenport, but, at that time, there was no bridge on which to cross. Fortunately, he arrived in very late December, and the river that year was covered with ice. For the third time (the first two at St. Louis) he walked across "Old Man River" on foot.

On New Years Eve that year, Emerson spoke at the Congregational Church in Davenport. The admission price was fifty cents. The event was not well-advertised, and the speaker was nonchalantly said to be an "essayist and poet."

We do not know what Emerson said, nor do we know the title, if there was one. A reporter in the audience said that the presentation confirmed that "[Emerson] writes and reasons well." At the same time, "he is *no* orator." He sauntered from topic to topic, the writer complained, such that his talk was not unlike the Laocoön Group, the famous Greek sculpture in which a man and his two sons are hopelessly entangled in a struggle with sea serpents.

AT THE TIME of that first Iowa talk, Emerson may still have been feeling the after effects of a courageous forthright statement he made some four years earlier.

In May of 1851, while speaking in Concord, Massachusetts, he had openly denounced the "fugitive slave law," which required citizens in the North not to impede but enable the capture of runaway slaves and their return to Southern enslavement.

In that speech, Emerson condemned the law as "one which every one of you will break on the earliest occasion" and "which no man can obey." It is a "filthy enactment," he wrote in his diary, "made in the nineteenth century by people who could read and write. I will not obey it." It is to Emerson's credit and to others of his time that the law was partly undermined.

As those opposed to slavery grew, personal liberty laws were passed, and there increased subversion through the Underground Railroad. To its credit, Iowa was among those states in which there was a network of safe houses for concealing fugitive slaves.

OF THOSE AT Emerson's Davenport talk in 1855, most were probably well aware of his opposition to slavery. Earlier, when Iowa had been granted statehood, its citizens had determined by vote that it should be a "free state," in which slavery would be banned.

In contrast, the bordering state of Missouri was pro-slavery. In 1859, shortly after Emerson's talk, the abolitionist John Brown and his colleagues (some of whom had secretly trained in Iowa) would mount their fateful failed attack on the Harpers Ferry Armory in Virginia. Soon enough, the bloody Civil War broke out.

Given those circumstances, Emerson did not return to Iowa until the Civil War had ended. He was once again invited to Davenport on January 19, 1866. His talk this time was well-received and reasonably well-attended, but the number was less than expected.

Because of bitter cold and winds, it was an "inauspicious night." From there, he traveled to Lyons to speak (now part of Clinton), then took a train to nearby DeWitt, where he was slated to appear at the Methodist Church at 7:30 pm on January 23.

ON THAT OCCASION, he reached his destination in ample time, but he was soon in a panic. He had not known the starting time of his talk, and he had reason to be concerned because his next appearance was scheduled for the following day in Dubuque.

In order to get there that evening, he would have to rush through his talk at DeWitt, so as not to miss the evening train. It was an awkward arrangement, as soon became apparent to the speaker and those in attendance.

Later, a DeWitt news report was blunt: Emerson was so openly worried about "making the train" that "he consulted his watch so frequently that it became a bore" to the audience.

Worse yet, "he thumbed over at least one half his manuscript unread," such that one might be led to suspect that his talk was a "genteel way of swindling people."

In the end, he did catch the train to Dubuque, where, on the following day, his talk was well-received. "Every sentence was a gem," a newspaper claimed. "When he had finished, one's brains felt like a tooth just filled—the gold crowded in and hammered down."

IN 1867, Emerson returned to Iowa, where he spoke in February at the Methodist Church in Washington, and the Baptist Church in Independence (reached by stage coach), where he spoke as a substitute for Horace Greeley (as in "Go West, young man!"), and from there to Cedar Falls. His remaining Iowa talks that trip were at Keokuk, Des Moines and Burlington.

He returned at the close of the same year to speak at Keokuk again. To get there from the Illinois side, he again crossed the Mississippi, but, too dangerous to walk across, he was transported in a skiff that was rowed across on the surface of the ice, since it was not reliably frozen.

He traveled west to speak again in Des Moines, and, on the return trip, he spoke in Davenport for the second time as well. Emerson's last talks in Iowa took place at the Athenaeum Theatre in Dubuque, on December 8, 1871, and, on the following Sunday, at the Unitarian Universalist Church.

Emerson was sixty-eight that year, and his public talks, as Hoeltje notes, were increasingly "a visible strain, for he seemed to hesitate more than formerly, as though he were overburdened with solicitude in his choice of words." He was experiencing memory loss and aphasia, and today, we might surmise that these were early indications of Alzheimer's or other dementia.

RETIRING TO his Concord home, the decline of his memory hastened. In his last years, there were times when he could not remember his name, and when asked how he was feeling, he would say, "I have lost my mental faculties, but I am perfectly well."

When he died of pneumonia in 1882, he was buried on "author's hill" in Concord's Sleepy Hollow Cemetery (not the earlier one in New York), near the graves of various friends, such as Nathaniel Hawthorne, Henry David Thoreau, and Louisa May Alcott. ■

HENRY DAVID THOREAU

I once had a sparrow alight upon my shoulder for a moment while I was hoeing in a village garden, and I felt that I was more distinguished by that circumstance than I should have been by an epaulet I could have worn.

Andrew Clemens (1883), sand bottle painting (two views) in tribute to Mary Heye. Collection of Smithsonian American Art Museum. Creative Commons.

SAND PAINTING
ON THE MISSISSIPPI

MARK TWAIN
The Mississippi River towns are comely, clean, well built, and
pleasing to the eye, and cheering to the spirit.

IN THE CLOSING year of World War I, a British-born American photographer named Arthur Mole succeeded in procuring 21,000 uniformed military personnel to stand still long enough that, from a distant elevated view, they appeared to form the profile of US President Woodrow Wilson.

Those in darker clothing became the president's hair, eye, and other features, while those dressed lighter seemed to be his skin, eyeglasses, shirt collar, and so on.

Most likely, readers will already know about Mole's famous photograph, since it appears so often on websites. That same year, he made other related images, such as a pastiche of the Liberty Bell that required 25,000 people to pose.

These are partly of interest because they are puns (one thing looks like something else), and partly because of the challenge of getting so many individuals to stand in one place long enough to take the photograph.

IN TRUTH, none of this was entirely new. There is an ancient tradition of arranging shapes in clusters to make them look like what they aren't, such as Arcimboldo's portraits.

There are also time-tested artists' techniques for hatching, cross-hatching, and stippling, by which images seem to consist of shades of gray, when in fact they were only printed in black.

With the invention of "half-tones" (a mechanical way of clustering and sizing dots to create the illusion of various grays), full-tone photographs could appear (using black ink only) in newspapers and magazines. With the arrival of color photographs, those too could soon be reproduced as half-tones, using over-printed clusters of dots in four ink colors.

Today, in the digital era, rectangular pixels have replaced dots, and as the pixels are enlarged, the effect looks increasingly jagged or blurred, in what is now commonly known as "pixelation."

BUT ALL THESE things had precedents, since artists had already commonly used small dabs of colored pigment to simulate effects of light.

That larger trend, as everyone knows, was called "Impressionism," while a variant using dots per se was "Pointillism." That the famous paintings of Georges Seurat and others anticipated "four-color process printing" can be seen by using a magnifying glass to look closely at a printed full-color image, to see that it consists of dots.

There are still other examples. Among the most familiar are charts for color blindness tests, in which numbers made of circular dots contrast with a background comprised of same-sized dots of differing hues. If stranded in the wilderness, we can use arrangements of rocks to spell out SOS.

In our own time, among those using such "grouping" techniques is a Brazilian artist named Vik Muniz, who has made compelling images from chocolate syrup, string, wire, dust or whatever. In one of his most astonishing works, he arranged thousands of Civil War soldiers and other plastic toys on a table top to replicate a portrait from a Mathew Brady photograph.

GRAINS OF SAND would also suffice. The technique of sand painting is, in fact, as old as the hills, in the sense that it has long been practiced by Navajo artists (using various colors of sand from their Southwest surroundings), Tibetan and Buddhist monks, and indigenous Australians.

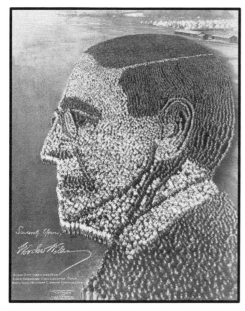

Arthur Mole and John Thomas (1918), uniformed servicemen assembled to look like a portrait of US President Woodrow Wilson. Public domain. Library of Congress Prints and Photographs.

In the second half of the 19th century, a curious variation emerged in eastern Iowa, in which designs with astonishing detail were made by arranging grains of colored sand from the bluffs of the Mississippi River.

To construct anything using only grains of sand is painstaking—but in this case the images were composed and tightly packed within glass jars designed for use by chemists. In ways, it was comparable to constructing a ship in a bottle, when building the ship would be challenge enough.

These sand art bottles were created between 1870 and 1894 by a self-taught "folk artist" from Iowa named Andrew Clemens. Born in 1857 in Dubuque, where his family remained only briefly, Clemens grew up in McGregor, Iowa, in the vicinity of Pikes Peak State Park, where there are astonishing overlooks of the Mississippi River.

AT THAT SITE, there is a region of sandstone called Pictured Rocks, where the sand has been naturally colored by the slow moist seepage of iron and other minerals. In some places, the colors have settled in one-color layers, while, in others, they are (as described in a news story) "mottled and variegated most fantastically."

As a youngster, Clemens' speech and hearing were impaired when stricken with encephalitis. In keeping with terminology then, he was described as "deaf and dumb." As a result, he spent his teenage years at the Iowa School for the Deaf in Council Bluffs, while returning home for summer breaks.

It was during those summers that he became intently interested in the colored sand deposits near McGregor. In 1877, when the school was closed because of a fire, he returned to his hometown, and remained there for the rest of his life. The only exception was a brief period around 1889, when he worked in Chicago as a "curiosity" at a popular museum. There, he made sand bottle paintings while museum visitors looked on.

CLEMENS IS USUALLY said to have made hundreds of sand bottle paintings in the years before his early death in 1894. But those that survive are considerably fewer in number.

To prevent any sand grains from shifting (as in Mole's large group photographs, each part must remain in place), the bottles' contents were extremely tightly packed, and sealed at the top with a stopper and wax. Thus sealed, care was required in viewing the art. A bottle might easily shatter if dropped, or break if two bottles collided—in which case the sand streamed out, and the pattern inside was completely destroyed.

Clemens' sand paintings were sought after while he was still living, and are even more coveted now (in a 2018 auction, one of his bottles sold for a record-breaking $132,000).

They are rare in part because a complex commission might require as long as a full year to complete. He was typically asked to make paintings that bore particular loved ones' names or played up themes at a client's request.

He was also beset by imitators, a few of whom had some success. But apparently no other artist was able to achieve the accuracy, detail, and intricacy of the sand bottle paintings by Clemens. Whereas his paintings might contain emblematic symbols, flags, birds, typographic components, ships, detailed architectural scenes, even George Washington on horseback, those by other sand artists (some of whom freely admitted that his work had inspired them) might be restricted to far less ambitious content.

One final bit of trivia: When you next find yourself engaged in conversation at a cocktail party, and the subject of sand art bottles comes up, you will no doubt amaze your friends if you mention that its technical name is *potichomanie*.

Good luck in pronouncing that. A double martini might actually help. ■

JONATHAN LYNN AND ANTONY JAY *Yes, Prime Minister*
So that means you need to know things even when you don't need to know them. You need to know them not because you need to know them but because you need to know whether or not you need to know. And if you don't need to know you still need to know so that you know that there was no need to know.

DONALD RUMSFELD US Defense Department briefing
As we know, there are known knowns; there are things we know we know. We also know that there are known unknowns, that is to say we know there are some things we do not know. But there are also unknown unknowns—the ones we don't know we don't know.

Anon, photograph of a Navajo man in the process of completing a sand painting by sprinkling colored sands. These were used in healing ceremonies, after which the elaborate painting was destroyed. Public domain.

LIVING AMONG
THE NAVAJO (DINÉ)

DESMOND TUTU referring to colonization in Africa
**When the missionaries came…they had the Bible and we had the land.
…We closed our eyes [in prayer]. When we opened them we had the
Bible and they had the land.**

FRANC JOHNSON NEWCOMB (née Frances Johnson) was born
in 1887 in the vicinity of Tomah, Wisconsin. Her father was an
architect, while her mother was a teacher at an area school that
included Native American children.

Orphaned before she reached her teens, Frances later
adopted the professional name of Franc, in tribute to her father.
In research publications, she is nearly always credited as Franc
Johnson Newcomb.

After high school, Franc remained in Wisconsin, and taught
Menominee children for several years at Keshena. In 1912, partly
for health reasons, she moved to the Southwest, where she
taught Navajo children at a government boarding school at Fort
Defiance, Arizona.

In one of her books, she remembers the reluctance of the
Native American students when she tried to teach them English.
The breakthrough came when she asked them to teach her
Navajo, in the process of which they themselves learned English.

AT FORT DEFIANCE, Franc met a young trader named Arthur J.
(called A.J.) Newcomb, who was from Manchester, Iowa. They
married in 1914, and went on to operate a trading post on the
Navajo Reservation in a remote, isolated region of New Mexico.

Its location was halfway between Gallup and Farmington, at a place now known as Newcomb. Their marriage continued for 32 years, during which they raised two daughters.

A.J. had purchased part of the trading post in 1913 and moved there to learn the business. One of the first Navajos to befriend him was Hosteen Klah, a prominent chanter, medicine man, and weaver.

When Franc arrived the following year as A.J.'s wife, she too became a close and long-term friend of Klah, and, fifty years later, she wrote a book about his life.

While respectful of the rituals and traditions of the Navajo, she also helped them cope with the diseases introduced by settlers. Often traveling to remote hogans to provide modern medicines, she became known as Atsay-Ashon or Medicine Woman.

HAVING GRADUALLY earned the trust of Klah and others, Franc was allowed to observe rituals that non-Indians had strictly been excluded from. These included sand painting ceremonies in which complex, colored patterns were painstakingly rendered in sand, then promptly destroyed at the end of the ceremony.

At first, as a silent observer, she memorized features of the sand paintings, then made drawings afterwards. "Since pencil, paper, or camera were not allowed in the lodge, I had only my memory to depend on," she later wrote, "…[but] In later years I trained myself to concentrate, and if allowed to remain in a ceremonial hogan for a half-hour, I could reproduce the painting without an error."

With Klah's and others' approval, she gained increasing access and was eventually permitted to record about 500 sand-paintings, which she recreated in paint on board. Some Navajos opposed this, condemning it as sacrilege, but Klah consented cautiously.

Forty-four of these were reproduced in her first book, *Sandpaintings of the Navajo Shooting Chant* (1937), while other paintings by her were preserved and are now exhibited at the Wheelwright Museum of the American Indian in Santa Fe.

Although she replicated scores of Navajo sand paintings, Franc did not regard herself as an "artist" in the usual sense. She was a writer and amateur ethno-anthropologist for whom her paintings were a reliable means of preserving sand painting tradition.

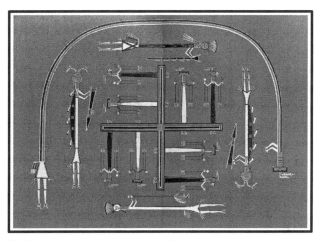

This is not a photograph of an actual Navajo sand painting, but of a painted replication of one, probably made by Franc Newcomb, as photographed by Horace Poley. Public domain.

She did this in other ways as well. For example, Hosteen Klah had been a weaver of Navajo rugs since the late 1880s. She asked if he might consider weaving monumental rugs (some as large as 12-foot square) that would replicate ceremonial sand paintings.

While reluctant at first, he eventually agreed, providing that they would be displayed respectfully as wall tapestries, not as rugs to be walked on.

KLAH'S FIRST SUCH tapestry was purchased by the wife of King Gillette, who had made a fortune from his invention of a razor with disposable blades, the iconic Gillette razor.

Above (top) is an undated photograph of Arthur and Franc Newcomb (fifth and sixth from left) in front of their trading post at Newcomb, New Mexico. Earle Newcomb is fourth from left, and Hosteen Klah is seated in the center, with a tapestry hanging on the right. Below that are two photographs (exterior and interior views) of the Wheelwright Museum, an elegant hogan-like structure. Public domain images.

His second tapestry was purchased by a wealthy heiress named Mary Cabot Wheelwright of Boston, who would establish the Wheelwright Museum in 1937. By the time of his death in that same year, Klah had woven twenty-five large tapestries, based on ceremonial sand paintings.

A few years later, Franc Johnson Newcomb published a book on *Navajo Omens and Taboos* (1940), and later co-authored *A Study of Navajo Symbolism* (1956). In 1964, when she authored a biography of Hosteen Klah, she dedicated it to the memory of her deceased former husband, Arthur John Newcomb, who had died in 1948. They had divorced two years earlier.

A decade prior to their divorce, A.J. was living at the trading post, while Franc was in Albuquerque, where their daughters were attending school. A news article described the devastating fire that destroyed their Newcomb compound (their home, the trading post, the manager's house, the camp cottages, and the garage) and most of their finest possessions that day. Insurance made it possible to rebuild part of the post, but the psychological damage was irreparable. According to one biographical source, "When fire destroyed their trading post in 1936, her husband's alcoholism became acute, straining [Franc] Newcomb to the breaking point." She moved permanently to Albuquerque, where she established a day-care center for children and a visiting nursing service.

At the same time, she became an active participant in the founding of the Wheelwright Museum (where much of her sand painting research is housed).

Funded by Mary Cabot Wheelwright, with Klah's consent, the hogan-like museum was designed by the well-known Southwest painter, designer, and architect William Penhallow Henderson, who had designed murals for Frank Lloyd Wright for the Midway Gardens in Chicago.

OF FRANC Johnson Newcomb's books, perhaps the finest is *Navajo Neighbors*, published in 1966, when she was nearly 80 years old. She would die just four years later.

That fascinating memoir, as Helen M. Bannon has noted, is "nonfiction prose blending history, autobiography, and folklore."

While some have dismissed Franc's research as amateur, Bannon concludes, others (such as Native American historian N. Scott Momady) have "applauded her realistic portrayals of Navajo life. To Newcomb, Navajos were people, not objects for study. This basic assumption permeates Newcomb's works, enhancing their value as a record of the personal dimension of intercultural communication." ■

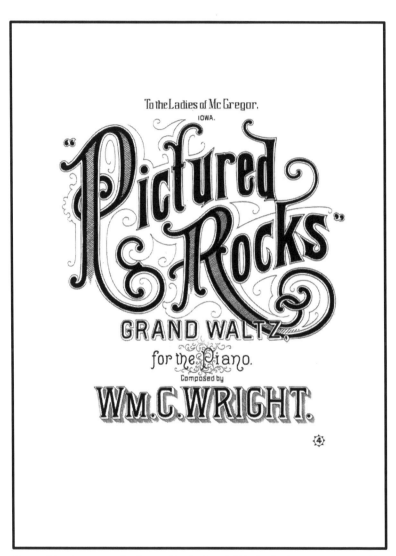

Cover of the sheet music for *Pictured Rocks Grand Waltz for the Piano*, as composed by William Cary Wright. Public domain.

SEARCHING FOR
FRANK LLOYD WRIGHT'S FATHER

CLAUDE DEBUSSY
Music is the arithmetic of sounds as
optics is the geometry of light.

WHEN JOHN LLOYD WRIGHT, son of the architect Frank Lloyd Wright, drafted a memoir about his life with his father, he asked him to read it and comment. In the requesting letter he wrote, "if you read it and come upon shadows, remember—sunshine made them."

When I first saw that sentence, I paused at the mention of shadows, because one of the things that is commonly said about the famous architect is that his accomplishments are of such splendor that anyone else's achievements are diminished by comparison. His was a blinding sunlight—while everyone else was left in the dark.

IN HIS book, Wright's son recalls the challenge he faced as a young architect, because he was often expected to be as masterful as his father. The situation was not helped when he changed his name, which was John Kenneth Wright at birth, to John Lloyd Wright. His older brother, also an architect, modified his name as well. He was Frank Lloyd Wright, Jr., at birth, but always used the professional name of Lloyd Wright.

There is a passage in John's book in which he lists the junior architects (five men, two women) who worked for his father in his Chicago studio. He admits that each of them, while working for

Wright, was "making valuable contributions to the pioneering of modern American architecture for which my father gets the full glory, headaches and recognition today!"

It is also commonly said that Frank Lloyd Wright changed his own birth name. According to legend (although it's sometimes questioned now), his original name was Frank Lincoln Wright, which seems not unreasonable, given Lincoln's recent death.

But years later, after Wright's parents separated, he changed his middle name to Lloyd, perhaps as a way to spurn his father, and to underscore his affinity with his mother's Welsh ancestors, the Lloyd Jones family. That family was famously prominent in a region of Wisconsin near Spring Green, where they owned a 600-acre estate called Jones Valley, which locals sardonically renamed "the valley of the God Almighty Joneses."

FRANK LLOYD WRIGHT'S mother, née Anna Lloyd Jones, was born in 1838. Her husband, the architect's father, William Cary Wright, was a Baptist minister who was born in 1825. So they differed in age by thirteen years.

At the time of their marriage in 1866, Wright's father had been a widower for two years, and was the single parent of three children, ages ten, eight and four. He brought these children into the marriage, and then, in successive years, he and his second wife (who was nearing thirty when they wed) went on to become the parents of three more children of their own: Frank Lloyd Wright and his two sisters.

Providing for that many children necessitates a substantial commitment, monetary and otherwise, especially if the income source is a spouse whose work is said to have been "itinerant," which means that he could be transferred. Within a span of seven years, William Wright served as a pastor in Wisconsin, Iowa, Rhode Island, and Massachusetts, before finally returning to settle in Wisconsin.

Given such frequent uprooting, perhaps we should not be surprised that the marriage only lasted about 15 years. In the past, the primary blame for the split-up has been attributed to Wright's father, whom his grandson John dismisses as "a Protestant preacher who excommunicated himself from several denominations, even from…his wife and children, and fled to— no one knows where."

THERE ARE, as is commonly noted, two sides to any story. And that is most likely the case in the unsuccessful marriage of Frank Lloyd Wright's parents.

This subject is rarely fully discussed, but little-known details began to emerge a half century ago, when a portion of a memoir by Frank Lloyd Wright's half-sister, Elizabeth Wright Heller (one of the children from William Cary Wright's first marriage), was published in March 1973 in the *Palimpsest* in Iowa. The entire 300-page typescript titled *The Story of My Life*, completed before Heller died in 1950, is in the collection of the State Historical Society of Iowa.

Since age 20, Heller had lived in the area of Marengo, Iowa, where she had worked as a milliner, typesetter, and teacher. In 1976, an account of the life of the father of Heller and her architect half-brother, Frank, was published in a book titled *Grandpa Wright* by Heller's great-granddaughter, Hope Sankot Rogers, who lived in Vinton, Iowa.

It was in part an exposé, in the sense that it contended that the failure of the marriage was as much the fault of Anna Lloyd Jones Wright as it was of William Cary Wright. In this and other sources about the story's "other side," not much good is said about Wright's mother, especially in connection with her treatment of her stepchildren.

"She was very sweet to us," Heller recalled, "[un]til after they were married." But it soon became apparent, as Anna's brother Jenkin agreed, that she was also capable of "a most tremendous temper."

"I was very much afraid of my stepmother," remembered Heller, "She not only beat me…but threatened me with some terrible things...I grew more and more afraid to be left alone with her."

The Wright-Jones marriage was a volatile blend. As Rogers' book concluded, it is hard to imagine two people who were more opposite, and "...it is not at all surprising that their marriage disintegrated. The marvel is that it lasted so long."

Anon, photographic view of downtown McGregor, Iowa (c1930). Public domain.

Rogers also made the case that Wright's father was not a ne'er-do-well drifter, as has often been supposed. He was a traveling preacher, but he had also studied law, literature, medicine, letterpress printing, and music in particular. He was a composer of music, and a performer and teacher as well. The music of Beethoven, Bach, Brahms, and others (which Wright's father introduced him to, as the architect admitted) was no less essential to Wright's approach to architecture than was his exposure to Froebel's kindergarten building blocks, which his mother brought home from the Centennial Exposition in Philadelphia in 1876.

THERE IS another component in this that prompted me to hesitate. It seems that William Cary Wright was small. He was short and slight of build. His feisty, strikingly beautiful wife was one head taller. But, as these revelations note, he was not nearly as small as his own father, also a preacher, who was too short to stand in the pulpit.

This is interesting in part because Frank Lloyd Wright is often said to have been short (in truth, he was about 5 feet 8 inches), and that it was that factor which prompted him to design residences in which the ceilings seem too low for some who visit them today.

But actually, the average height of American men has increased over the past century. In Wright's era, the average man was 5 feet 7 inches (so Wright was no shorter than average), whereas by 2016 the average height had increased to 5 feet 10 inches.

After his parents' separation and divorce, Wright never saw his father again, and he all but never mentioned his estranged half-siblings in the later published accounts of his life. William Cary Wright died in 1904, having resettled just west of Omaha, Nebraska, where he established a sheet music publishing firm, and where he could be close to relatives from his first marriage.

In 1928, when Hope Rogers was four years old, the famous (and infamous) Frank Lloyd Wright showed up at a reunion at the Sankot family farm near Belle Plaine, Iowa. Wright's half-sister, Elizabeth Wright Heller, was also present, at which time she was 68. It is said that their meeting was cordial, if not entirely, and it may have been the final time that descendants of the marriage met. The "prodigal son" had been greatly delayed in returning—and the enmity was soon restored. ■

SYDNEY SMITH

[Marriage is] A pair of sheers, so joined that they cannot be separated: often moving in opposite directions, yet always punishing anyone who comes between them.

Anon, portrait photograph of Samuel Langhorne Clemens, aka Mark Twain (1907).
Library of Congress Prints and Photographs.

A TALE OF TWAIN WIVES

ALAN WATTS
Reality is only
a Rorschach inkblot, you know.

MARK TWAIN, the pen name of Samuel Langhorne Clemens, was born in November 1835, coincident with the arrival of Haley's Comet. That spectacular event occurs about every 75 years, and, in April 1910, when Clemens was on his deathbed, he and the comet crossed paths again.

At the moment of Clemens' death, among those at his bedside was Albert Bigelow Paine. A prominent writer, Paine was a close associate of Clemens, who had chosen him to write his biography and to serve as his literary executor.

Three months later, a newspaper in Keokuk, Iowa, reported that Paine had been visiting that city, gathering information for his biography of Clemens. "It is not generally known," the article said, "that the first literary efforts of Mark Twain were for a Keokuk paper. He worked with his brother in a printing shop on Third Street."

WHAT THE ARTICLE failed to mention is that Paine himself had Iowa roots. During the American Civil War, Paine and his parents had lived in Bentonsport, Iowa, near Keosauqua, on the Des Moines River, in the southeast region of the state. His father, Captain Samuel Estabrook Paine, was a Union officer, and the commander of Company I of the 19th Iowa Infantry.

The elder Paine had led his unit in Arkansas in the Battle of Prairie Grove, on December 7, 1862, about ten miles from Fayetteville. Captain Paine was wounded that day, and was discharged the following year, because of disabilities. At the time of the battle, his son was still an infant. After the father returned home to Iowa, the family moved to Xenia, Illinois, where young Albert attended school, and where their historic home still stands.

During his life as a writer, Albert Bigelow Paine not only authored a five-volume biography of Mark Twain, he published four other books about him, including his letters and speeches. He also wrote other biographies, children's books, novels, travel books, and books of poetry, including humorous verse. He was also a member of the Pulitzer Prize Committee.

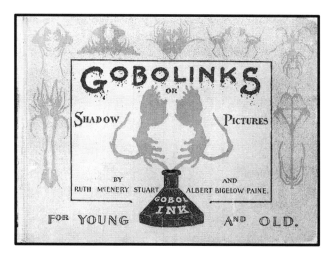

PAINE'S MOST unusual achievement may be his co-authorship, with Ruth McEnery Stuart, of a book of "klecksographic images" (pictures made from inkblots), juxtaposed with humorous verse.

The book's title, *Gobolinks or Shadow Pictures for Young and Old* (1896), is a merger by portmanteau of "goblin" and "ink." On the cover is a bottle of ink that bears the label *Gobol Ink*.

The German word for an inkblot is *klecks*. In the latter half of the nineteenth century, it was a source of amusement to drop ink on a scrap of paper, then fold the paper to produce a bilaterally symmetrical "picture."

If this at once reminds you of the famous Rorschach Inkblot Test developed by Swiss psychiatrist Hermann Rorschach, you are precisely on target. This pastime had been commonplace during Rohrschach's childhood, and he was preoccupied with it—so much so that his classmates called him *Klex* (or inkblot).

YEARS EARLIER, a German doctor named Justinus Kerner had used comparable inkblots to inspire a book of poems. French psychologist Alfred Binet, who devised the IQ test, was also fascinated by inkblots, as was the writer Victor Hugo, who made

Cover (far left) of Ruth McEnery Stuart and Albert Bigelow Paine, *Gobolinks or Shadow Pictures for Young and Old* (1896). Inkblot insects (left) by Justinus Kerner (c1890). Public domain.

countless "accidental" images, combining chimerical inkblots with coffee stains, wine, and soot.

Paine and Stuart surely must have been aware of some of these earlier experiments. At one point there was even a popular game called *Klexographie* or *Blotto*.

When they produced their book in 1896, they shared a procedure by which it too could be a game. Each player had a limited time in which to make a "gobolink," using ink and folded paper, and then write a verse to go with it.

IF IMITATION is the sincerest form of flattery, the co-authors must have been swollen with pride when, just eleven years after the release of *Gobolinks*, an author named John Prosper Carmel produced a disarmingly similar book (albeit not as good as theirs) of inkblot images and poems, titled *Blottentots, and How to Make Them* (Paul Elder and Company, 1907).

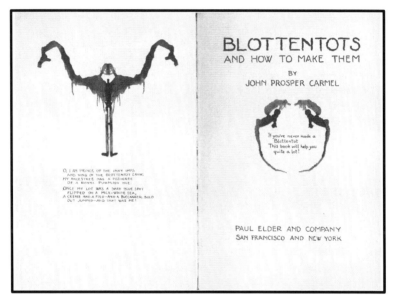

Title spread of John Prosper Carmel, *Blottentots and How to Make Them* (1907). Public domain.

The book's hand lettering is attributed to a book illustrator named Raymond Carter, and there is speculation that Carmel was his pseudonym. Carmel's book was warmly received by reviewers, as in *Goodwin's Weekly*, in which it was described as "a whole menagerie" of "startling, ludicrous, haphazard, jackadandies—the funniest that ever jumped out of paper—a jolly jingle with each, and full instructions in rhyme for making others just as funny."

The instructions in Carmel's book, unlike Paine and Stuart's, are themselves jolly jingles, as in this example:

> Don't crease exactly at the blot—
> You'll have a fearful muddle;
> Press gently, too, and not a lot,
> Unless you want a puddle.

For the moment, we need to go back to Albert Bigelow Paine, Mark Twain's biographer and the co-author of *Gobolinks*. From all that has been said thus far, it seems he led a virtuous life that was free of any behavioral taints.

That said, it is with some regret to note that a 2018 article in the *Mark Twain Journal* reports otherwise. Titled "Biographer Obscura: The Secret Life of Albert Bigelow Paine," the article's author, Max McCoy, documents his discovery that Paine may have been a bigamist—that he married twice, that he wed his second wife (the daughter of his dentist) without having divorced the first, that he fathered one daughter by his first wife and two daughters by the second, and that none of the children were told of their father's bilateral wives.

They had not so much as an inkling. ■

PHILIPPE BURTY quoted in *Shadows of a Hand*
Any means [of drawing] would do for him [Victor Hugo], the dregs of a cup of coffee tossed on old laid paper, the dregs of an inkwell tossed on notepaper, spread with his fingers, sponged up, dried, then taken up with a thick brush or a fine one...Sometimes the ink would bleed through the notepaper, and so on the reverse another vague drawing was born.

Zaida Ben-Yusuf (c1900), portrait photograph of Elbert Hubbard. Public domain. Wikimedia Commons.

ARTS, CRAFTS,
SCANDAL, SUDDEN DEATH

WILLIAM MORRIS
I do not want art for a few any more than education
for a few, or freedom for a few.

IN 1887, twenty-six-year-old Alice Moore resigned as a primary school teacher in Cedar Falls, Iowa, and returned to the region in which she was raised. She accepted a high school teaching post in East Aurora, New York, just outside of Buffalo.

In later years, until her tragic death in 1915, Alice Moore would become known as a writer, a suffragette, and a feminist. Of particular impact was her collaborative work with her husband, a writer and ersatz philosopher named Elbert Hubbard.

Working together in East Aurora, they headed an arts and crafts community called Roycroft, a project partly inspired by the example of William Morris and the British Arts and Crafts Movement.

HUBBARD HIMSELF was a Midwesterner, having grown up near Chicago. As a young man, he had been highly successful as a traveling salesman for the Larkin Soap Company.

His innovative sales techniques (premiums, product trials, and mail order sales) were widely adopted, and the company thrived.

As it expanded, the Larkin Company moved east to Buffalo. Hubbard acquired a third of the firm, and became the second in command. But, as the years passed, he increasingly felt unchallenged, and began to imagine a writing career. In 1893, he retired from the company, with a settlement of about two million dollars (approximate current value).

His departure was not entirely smooth, even though two of his sisters were married to Larkin executives. He may have played a backstage role in the choice of Frank Lloyd Wright (whom he had known in Chicago) as the architect for the company's administrative center, the famous Larkin Building.

HUBBARD'S WIFE, Bertha Crawford Hubbard, did not oppose his change to a writing career, and in 1895, they launched a private printing firm, called Roycroft Press (in tribute to Morris' Kelmscott Press). It was Bertha who designed the title page of their first book, *The Song of Songs*.

That initial endeavor, which resulted in periodicals called *The Philistine* and *The Fra*, and a series of biographical essays called *Little Journeys*, was the first phase in the founding of the Roycroft community.

A phenomenal change in their fortune occurred in 1899, when Hubbard published a story in *The Philistine* about worker initiative and corporate loyalty, titled *A Message to Garcia* (which he claimed he had written in a half hour).

When reprinted in book form, millions of copies were sold (possibly as many as forty million), in part because companies bought them to distribute to their workers. Soon Hubbard was a household name, and was increasingly in demand as an inspirational speaker.

HUBBARD HAD grown up in Bloomington, Illinois, but he had never crossed the Mississippi until he lectured at Brown's Opera House in Waterloo, Iowa, on January 15, 1900.

His Iowa tour then continued to Cedar Falls, Fort Dodge, Cedar Rapids, Des Moines, and New Hartford. His talks were inevitably well-received, and in October of the same year, he was invited by a friend (Cedar Falls school superintendent O.J. Laylander) to return as the main attraction at the annual meeting of the Northeastern Iowa Teachers Association in Clinton.

Two years later, he spoke in November at the opera house in Algona, Iowa, where the tickets sold out in two hours.

The following month, an article in the *Waterloo Courier* revealed that Elbert and Bertha Hubbard had been living separate lives for more than a year. She had filed for divorce (with adultery as the reason) and negotiations about alimony and child support were on-going (wed in 1881, the Hubbards had raised three sons).

Dard Hunter (1914), design for title spread of Elbert Hubbard, *So Here Cometh Pig-Pen Pete*, published by Roycroft Press. Public domain.

AS THE STORY unfolded, it was revealed that Elbert Hubbard had fallen in love with Alice Moore (the Iowa teacher who had moved back to East Aurora in 1887).

They had embarked on a drawn-out secret affair, which continued, off and on, sometimes by trysts, more often by impassioned letters. Surely, for everyone involved, the point of no return occurred in the latter half of the 1890s, when Hubbard fathered one daughter (Miriam) by his mistress, and concurrently fathered a second (Katherine) by his wife.

The stigma of being an unwed mother would have ruined

Alice Moore's life. She could never again work as a teacher. As a result, the daughter that Alice gave birth to was quietly raised for the first six years by Alice's sister and husband in Buffalo.

Miriam grew up initially believing that her birth mother was instead her visiting aunt. In 1904, when Elbert Hubbard and Alice Moore were finally able to marry, they settled in East Aurora, along with their reclaimed daughter, who was eight years old by then.

Elbert and Alice Hubbard, with their daughter Miriam. Public domain.

IN SUBSEQUENT years, Alice took over much of the management of the Roycroft community, in part because Elbert continued to tour as a public speaker.

The fame of the Roycroft colony grew, thanks to the ubiquity of its publications, but also because its line of products enlarged to include not just letterpress printing, but affordable, sturdy Arts and Crafts chairs, lamps, clocks and other furniture, metalworking, leather craft, and bookbinding.

By 1910, the colony had grown to nearly 500 resident workers, with fourteen buildings on what was known as the "Roycroft campus."

As Hubbard continued to travel the country as a "platform speaker," he returned to Iowa now and then. In 1906, he spoke at the Burtis Opera House in Davenport; at the Methodist Episcopal Church in Bloomfield in 1904; in Waterloo in 1913; and at the Advertising Club in Cedar Rapids in 1914.

At some point, he met and developed a friendship with B.J. Palmer, whose family had established the Palmer School of Chiropractic (PSC) in Davenport.

In emulation of Hubbard, Palmer set up his own Palmer Print Shop, made use of marketing techniques that were modeled after Hubbard's, collected Roycroft books and furniture, and even dressed like "Fra Elbertus," wearing long hair, a headband, and a flowing Buster Brown cravat (as did Oscar Wilde, Frank Lloyd Wright, Walter Burley Griffin, and other "aesthetes" of the time).

IN 1915, at the height of the popularity of the Roycroft Community, Elbert and Alice tragically died. The United States had not yet entered World War I, and, on May 1, they boarded the RMS *Lusitania* at New York, for the purpose of visiting England, as well as parts of Europe, to appeal to all for a mutual peace.

They were onboard on May 7, when the famous passenger ship was struck by a German torpedo. 1,198 people perished, and the Hubbards were among the American citizens killed.

They might have survived, but, according to witnesses, when last seen, they made no effort to be saved, but instead stood calmly holding hands, resigned to the fate of their drowning.

The Hubbards' bodies were lost at sea. It is an uncanny addition to note that, five weeks after the Hubbards' death, the *Waterloo Courier* published a news article in which a Waterloo resident named George H. Wilson (who until recently had lived and worked at the Roycroft Colony in East Aurora) claimed to have Elbert Hubbard's suitcase, recovered from the ship's debris.

The battered container, the article states, "is on display in a window on the Fourth Street side of the Black Hawk Building [in Waterloo], and is attracting interested crowds." ■

Unknown photographer, Le Corbusier at Shodhan House in India (1955). Public domain. Wikimedia Commons.

OCCUPANT OF A HOUSE BY LE CORBUSIER

CICELY GITTES Interview

I remember that Cook was always very nice about Le Corbusier, and I have an idea that Le Corbusier was rather a stinker.

THE FRENCH WORD for raven (as well as for certain crows) is *corbeau*. Around 1920, the Swiss-French architect Charles-Edouard Jeanneret (1887-1965) adopted the pseudonym Le Corbusier as a way to allude to the annual task of his forebears during the Middle Ages of cleaning out nests of crows and other birds from the local church steeple.

Le Corbusier went on to become one of the most celebrated architects of the 20th century. But what is less commonly known is that one of his early clients was an Iowa-born expatriate artist named William Edwards Cook (1881-1959), for whom he designed an innovative four-level home called Villa Cook (or Maison Cook) on the outskirts of Paris.

WILLIAM EDWARDS COOK, a painter, was born and raised in Independence, the county seat of Buchanan County in northeast Iowa. Inspired by the paintings of J.M.W. Turner and by John Singer Sargent (whom some have claimed he actually met), he left home at age 18 to study art in Chicago and New York, then moved to Paris in 1903.

Several years later, while visiting Rome, he became the first American artist to be invited to paint a portrait of Pope Pius X. It was while living in Paris that Cook became closely acquainted with the American writer Gertrude Stein, who invited him to gatherings on Saturday evenings at her home at 27 rue de Fleurus.

It was at those gatherings that he met dozens of now famous Modernists, among them Stein's companion, Alice B. Toklas, the dancer Isadora Duncan, the writer Ernest Hemingway, and the artists Pablo Picasso, Henri Matisse, and Jacques Lipchitz.

COOK MARRIED his Breton-born French wife, named Jeanne Moallic, after living together for nearly a decade. Over the years, Stein and Toklas became close friends with Cook and Jeanne. As described in Stein's autobiographies (*The Autobiography of Alice B. Toklas* and *Everybody's Autobiography*), the two couples vacationed together several times on the Spanish island of Mallorca, where Stein and Cook especially enjoyed the bullfights, but which Alice and Jeanne found disturbing.

While working as a taxi driver in Paris, Cook taught Gertrude Stein to drive, so that, during World War I, she and Toklas could distribute supplies for the American Fund for French Wounded. "Cook does and he says and he is kind to all," Stein wrote admiringly of her friend. "He understands all. He is so kind."

After the war, Cook spent three years in the Caucasus, aiding refugees in the aftermath of the Russian Revolution, while working on the record for the Red Cross, but most likely also spying for the American government.

COOK'S FATHER, an Iowa lawyer and landowner named Justin Cook, died in 1924. Cook used part of his inheritance to buy land and build a home in Boulogne sur Seine. While searching for an architect, he was introduced to the then obscure Le Corbusier by the sculptor Jacques Lipchitz, who had just had a similar villa designed by the architect in the same area.

At the same time, with some hesitation, Le Corbusier also agreed to design a villa for Michael Stein, Gertrude's older brother. The architect was hesitant because the Steins had furnished their previous home with Italian Renaissance antiques.

"Don't buy anything but practical furniture and never decorative furniture," Le Corbusier advised. And, as he explained to Michael Stein, "I have to be very careful when I take [on] my clients so that they won't spoil my house with their furniture."

Gertrude Stein and Alice B. Toklas in New York, at the time of their arrival in the US (1933). Public domain.

THE FIRST FORMAL meeting between the Cooks and Le Corbusier took place on April 28, 1926. They must have had few disagreements because the basic plan for the house was completed only three days later, on May 1, and the layout was fundamentally the same when the actual construction began in July of that year.

In contrast, a series of major revisions were made in the design of the Michael Stein villa, so that construction of that project had still not begun when the Cooks moved into their finished home in March of 1927.

This is not to say that everything went smoothly in the construction of Villa Cook. In early September, for example, Cook discovered that Le Corbusier (whom he described in a letter as a "temperamental genius") had mistakenly placed the house beyond his property line, 50 centimeters into his neighbor's land.

"I thought this was a thing that was not according to Hoyle," Cook wrote to Gertrude Stein, "and he [Le Corbusier] told me I seemed to be a type absolutely without gratitude. Gratitude be damned says I—What I want is to have the thing fixed up. Well, it will cost me 10,000 francs before the thing is finished and he is mad because I have no appreciation of the fact that he got me 50 centimeters of land I didn't want."

Several months later, there was yet another annoying confusion between architect and client. The former may have deliberately underestimated the cost of the project at its outset, in part by allowing for certain details (such as the quality of the window glass) to be decided later.

While the architect was on vacation, it was Cook who apparently chose to install regular window glass in the windows on the street facade of the building, instead of heavier plate glass. When the architect returned, he sent Cook a letter demanding a correction: "I am convinced that you will readily agree to it so as to avoid a serious blemish to your property,"wrote Le Corbusier.

He continued: "For you we have made the best of our houses, and one with which we have taken particular trouble. Alas, I fear that you do not appreciate it for what it is, or the distressing incidents which you have caused us would not have happened."

After all, he added, "A fine gentleman setting out for a ball would never wear a paper collar with his dinner jacket."

LE CORBUSIER'S early buildings are often described as the architectural equivalent of Cubist paintings, and he himself described Villa Cook as "the true cubic house" (*le vrai maison cubique*). The structure is a literal cube in the sense that the plan and elevation are both derived from the same square.

The ground level of Villa Cook is divided into a car port on one side, and a pedestrian entrance and walkway on the other. Raised above ground by *pilotis* (or stilts) and side walls, the living quarters are housed in a sculptural two-story box, with a curiously inverted room arrangement:

The bedrooms, dressing room, bathroom, and the original maid's room are all on the first floor; while the kitchen, dining room, and living room are on the second. The height of the living room is double, so that it flows up into the fourth level, which contains a roof garden and library.

Shortly after his clients moved into their new home, Le Corbusier sent a vase of flowers to Mrs. Cook. To which Cook responded that "We are more and more pleased with the house day by day."He continued: "Mrs. Cook was delighted with the superb arrangement of flowers which she received yesterday evening. The living room is full of them, like a field in springtime."

Jeanne Cook added: "We are very happy and grateful that you have managed to produce not only a great house, but a very pretty one, with so much light and sunshine."

While undoubtedly pleased with their home, the Cooks asked that it be modified several years later by the addition of a separate maid's quarters in the rear, with an outdoor bedroom and recreation area on the floor above.

The Cooks recommended Le Corbusier to prospective clients, and occasionally showed the interior to acquaintances who were planning to build a house.

As one of Gertrude Stein's friends, William G. Rogers, remarked in his memoir, *When This You See Remember Me: Gertrude Stein In Person*, Cook was important at the time not as an artist but "largely as the occupant of a house built by Le Corbusier....")

COOK AND JEANNE moved out of Villa Cook in 1934. While continuing to own the house, they leased it when they lived briefly in Rome and then settled permanently on Mallorca off the coast of Spain. As they aged, they talked about where they should live in retirement.

Railway station at Independence, Iowa. Library of Congress. Public domain.

"Have told Jeanne that if she prefers we can go and live in Iowa,"Cook wrote to Gertrude Stein, but "she seems to have leanings toward Palma [de Mallorca], as I have myself." He added: "She says she likes Iowa, but has the feeling that Paddy [their dog] would not be happy there..."

In October of the same year, Gertrude Stein and Alice B. Toklas sailed to America for a six-month book promotion tour. Among their scheduled appearances was a lecture at the Times Literary Club in Iowa City, on the second floor of what is now the Prairie Lights Bookstore.

"Is that anywhere near [his hometown of] Independence?" Stein asked Cook in a letter. "We would love to lecture in Independence but I am afraid it is too far away. It almost feels to us like a home tour." In the end, even her Iowa City lecture was cancelled when her plane was forced to land in Waukesha, Wisconsin, because of a terrible snowstorm.

"I WOULD LIKE to have seen Iowa," Stein recalled later in *Everybody's Autobiography*. "Carl [Van Vechten, the music critic] and Cook come from Iowa, you are brilliant and subtle if you come from Iowa and really strange and you live as you live and you are always well taken care of if you come from Iowa."

William Edwards Cook died in Mallorca in 1959 at age 78, while Jeanne died two years later. They were buried in a small cemetery in Genova, on the outskirts of Palma de Mallorca.

Surviving both is Villa Cook at 6 rue Denfert Rochereau in Boulogne sur Seine, which was described in recent years in an architectural directory as "almost in original state" and only "slightly worn."

The building's reputation has also survived: While never regarded as a major work by Le Corbusier, it is frequently cited as the first implementation of what he and his cousin and architectural partner (Pierre Jeanneret) defined as the "Five Points of a New Architecture." ■

SAMUEL PUTNAM *Paris Was Our Mistress*

[Remembering]...the prairies, that endless waving sea of green in summer, in other seasons an expanse of brown stubble or of snow. But flat, always flat! Anyone who has not been born and reared in the heart of the prairies will never be able to appreciate how intensely a boy can long for the sight of a mountain or for a glimpse of lake, sea, or river, something more than the dirty little half dried-up creek that ran through the scant woods on the outskirts of the central Illinois village where I was born and where I lived until my late teens.

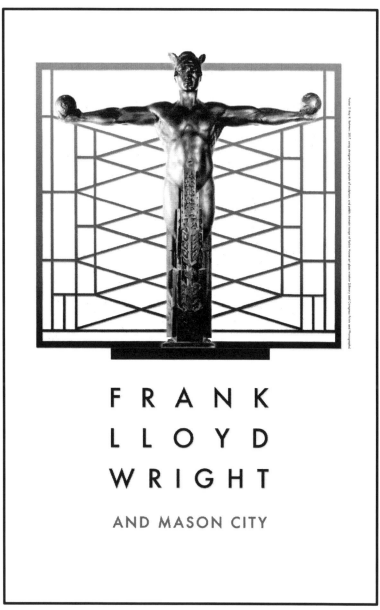

FRANK
LLOYD
WRIGHT
AND MASON CITY

Roy R. Behrens, from a series of commemorative posters on Frank Lloyd Wright and Mason City (2015).

FLATLANDERS
GO DOWN UNDER

JOHN RUSKIN
No person who is not a great sculptor or painter can be an architect.
If he is not a sculptor or painter, he can only be a *builder*.

A FEW YEARS AGO, while lecturing in Australia, I was not at all surprised to find that most of the people I spoke to were well aware of Frank Lloyd Wright. I was surprised, however, by the number of those who also knew about Mason City, Iowa.

They had heard of Mason City (and some had even visited there) because of its connection with Wright. In 1907, he was commissioned by Mason City attorneys to design a multi-purpose building that could house a bank, hotel, law offices, shops, and rental spaces.

The two primary components would be the City National Bank, which faced a bustling downtown street, and the Park Inn, which looked out on a tranquil park.

The Australians also knew that Wright, while working on that larger project (begun in 1909), had adapted an earlier plan for a Prairie style home for a local physician named Stockman. The prototype plan for the structure had been published in 1907 in the *Ladies Home Journal*. Now known as the Stockman House, that residence was completed in 1908.

TWO YEARS LATER, when the City National Bank and Park Inn opened with a festive ceremony, Frank Lloyd Wright did not attend. In all likelihood, he was not invited to return.

Wright had left for Germany the year before, after newspapers widely reported his amorous liaison with the wife of a Chicago client and his abandonment of his own wife and children.

Had Wright not been sullied by scandal, he probably would have been hired by Mason City businessmen to design an entire neighborhood on facing sides of Willow Creek in what is now referred to as the Rock Crest-Rock Glen Historic District.

Instead, the commission was offered to Walter Burley Griffin, one of Wright's young associates in his Chicago architectural firm. It was a wise decision to offer the commission to Griffin. Or so it seemed initially.

AS A TALENTED architect with a particular interest in landscape design, Griffin's skills were well-suited for designing innovative homes within a planned surrounding.

He initially proposed that there would be as many as 19 unique single-family residences in the Rock Crest-Rock Glen neighborhood. But the project never reached that goal—only seven houses were completed, and only five were his designs. In part, the project was never completed because of Griffin's capabilities as an architect—he was, in a way, too good. And Australia played a central role.

After initial long distance discussions with his Mason City clients, Griffin traveled there from Chicago in 1912 to look at the natural setting and develop a suitable plan.

As he began to work intently on the buildings and surroundings for Rock Crest–Rock Glen, he was also preparing an entry for an international contest to design the buildings and surrounds of Canberra, the new capital of Australia.

HIS COLLABORATOR in this was Marion Mahony (a remarkable draftsman and designer herself and one of the country's first women architects), whom he had married the year before, and who, along with Griffin, had been a longtime associate in Wright's architectural office.

Meanwhile the on-site negotiations with his Mason City clients could hardly have been more successful. Not only was consensus reached about the layout of the neighborhood, but Griffin also delivered the plans for four of the residences: the Harry D. Page house, Arthur L. Rule house, James E. Blythe house, and Joshua G. Melson house.

All four structures were innovative and unique, but the Melson House (on the Rock Crest side) is by far the most peculiar. It stands tall unabashedly at the top of an imposing limestone bluff, made of the very same stone it appears to have arisen from. Embedded yet conspicuous, its presence cannot be ignored. From the beginning, townspeople have referred to it as "the castle."

But complications soon arose, because, in May of 1912, Griffin's submission for the design of the Australian capital (in which Marion Mahony Griffin played a significant part) was awarded the top prize from among 137 proposals. He would soon be required to visit the site.

IN AUGUST 1913, a 30-page sequence of drawings and photographs of his work (including his Mason City designs) was published in *Western Architect*, followed by an article in *Architectural Review*.

The Griffins traveled to Australia for the first time in August, then returned in November to work on a plan to transfer the responsibility of completing the Rock Crest–Rock Glen project. When the Griffins left for Australia again in 1914, they had no idea that they (as a couple) would never return.

World War I would soon begin, and the political disagreements about the architectural plans for Canberra were nearly as deadly as warfare itself.

Today, more than a century later, Frank Lloyd Wright's City National Bank and Park Inn have been miraculously restored as

Roy R. Behrens, commemorative posters (above and left) from a series on Frank Lloyd Wright and Mason City architecture (2015).

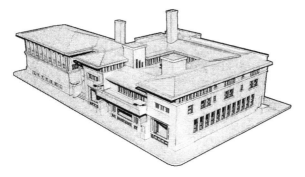

Author's digital rendering of a scale model of Frank Lloyd Wright's
City National Bank and Park Inn in Mason City, Iowa.

the Historic Park Inn, and the Stockman House is a museum.

In recent years, the city has been named by *Condé Nast Traveler* magazine as one of the top destinations worldwide for architectural devotees. And the astonishing (if less famous) contributor to that notoriety is the Griffins' Rock Crest-Rock Glen neighborhood, which—by itself—is worth the trip. ■

GUY MURCHIE *Song of the Sky*
Clouds are the sheet music of the heavens, the architecture of moving air...some are ragged coattails of storms that have passed. Some are stagnant blankets of warm air resting on cold. Some are mare's tails floating in the chill upper sky. Some are herringbones, sheets, cream puffs, ox-bends, veils, hammerheads, spangled mantillas, sponges, black shrouds.

Sherry Edmundson Fry, statue of Chief Mahaska (1907), Native American tribal leader, located in the town square in Osklaloosa, Iowa. Public domain image.

SHERRY FRY AND
THE BIRTH OF CAMOUFLAGE

ALFRED E. CORNEBISE *Art from the Trenches*
Bt war's end, more than three thousand French artists of all ages and artistic schools had served the nation [as camouflage artists].

THE CITY OF Oskaloosa in southeastern Iowa is the county seat of Mahaska County. In the town square is an elegant bronze statue of Chief Mahaska, the 19th-century leader of a tribe of Native Americans known as the Ioways.

At the right of the base of the statue is the signature "S.E. Fry, 1907." He was Sherry Edmundson Fry, an American sculptor who was born in Creston, Iowa, on September 29, 1879.

At the turn of the century, he studied sculpture at the Art Institute of Chicago with Lorado Taft, and in Paris with Frederick McMonnies, a student of Augustus Saint-Gaudens.

At the beginning of his career, Fry won several international competitions, including the Prix de Rome, and, as a result of that, received a number of public and private commissions, among them a pediment for the Frick Museum in New York City, reliefs for the Grant Memorial in Washington, DC, and the fountain at St. George on Staten Island. The statue of Mahaska was Fry's first commission.

Funded by James Depew Edmundson of Des Moines, it was in part a memorial to Edmundson's father, William Edmundson, who had worked closely with the Ioways as the first sheriff of Mahaska County.

Having accepted the commission, Fry returned to Iowa from

Paris, to make drawings of Native Americans at the settlement at Tama, and to create a clay scale model of the statue. The final full-sized bronze was cast in Paris and exhibited briefly at the Louvre, before being shipped to Iowa.

FRY'S ACHIEVEMENTS as a sculptor are all but completely forgotten today. In addition, virtually no one remembers or cares that, during World War I, he was one of the founders of the American Camouflage Corps, an organization of dozens of artists who volunteered for military service as camouflage experts.

When the US entered World War I in 1917, Fry (who lived in New York at the time) approached a friend with a news photograph of French camouflage. That friend was an American painter named Barry Faulkner, who had studied with Saint-Gaudens, and the photograph, Faulkner remembered, was of "a French train and railway station painted in bold disrupted patterns."

Fry showed Faulkner the photograph because the latter was a cousin and former student of Abbott H. Thayer, a prominent New Hampshire painter who had published an important book on animal camouflage in 1909.

In *Concealing Coloration in the Animal Kingdom*, Thayer ("the father of camouflage") had claimed that brightly-colored and distinctively patterned animals are sometimes better camouflaged than those that are plain and earth-colored. The photograph that Fry showed to Faulkner depicted an attempt by French artists to apply Thayer's principle of surface disruption to military field camouflage.

Two years earlier, the French had created the first camouflage unit in military history. The founder and leader of this *section de camouflage* was a painter, and nearly all *les camoufleurs* in the French Army were artists of one kind or another, including painters, sculptors, cartoonists, architects and stage designers. Later, the British army and navy used artists and others to form various camouflage units.

If the US was going to take part in the war, reasoned Fry and Faulkner, perhaps American artists should voluntarily set up their own camouflage unit. To promote this idea, Fry and Faulkner organized meetings of New York artists and architects, and, using Faulkner's relation to Thayer as "bogus prestige," met with prominent military and political figures.

"We knew nothing about war," Faulkner later confessed, "and very little about practical camouflage; but it was an outlet for our excitement." Their efforts proved futile in certain ways, successful in others.

AS IT HAPPENED, the US government did establish an infantry Camouflage Corps in 1917, and Fry and Faulkner were among its first members.

However, the artists in charge of the group were a New York architect named Everett Tracy and a freshly-trained lieutenant from New Hampshire named Homer Saint-Gaudens, who was Faulkner's former roommate at Harvard and the son of Augustus Saint-Gaudens. In addition, other Iowans, both artists and scientists, contributed to the development of WWI camouflage, among them Grant Wood, Carol Sax, and Mathew Luckiesh.

Initially housed on the campus of George Washington University, the Camouflage Corps practiced drills and calisthenics in the morning, then hiked and experimented with camouflage in the afternoon.

For publicity, they camouflaged their own barracks, and, under Fry's direction, they "painted cars and trucks in disruptive patterns; constructed papier-mâché dummies of fallen tree-trunks from whose interiors an unseen sniper could shoot; and dug trenches covered with so and bushes from which soldiers could pop out and discomfit the enemy."

In November 1917, Company A of the 40th Engineers (the unit's official designation) demonstrated camouflage for an audience that included President Woodrow Wilson and the

American painter John Singer Sargent. As part of the demonstration, Fry had concealed a sniper in a papier-mâché tree trunk, a deception so effective that the President praised him for "the quality and ingenuity of his work."

TWO MONTHS LATER, on New Year's Day, the Camouflage Corps set sail for France. Arriving at the French harbor of Brest, Faulkner remembered: "We saw that camouflage had preceded us, for the harbor was full of boats, both French and American, painted in a riot of disruptive patterns." The riotous patterns that Faulkner observed were examples of what was then commonly called "dazzle painting" (which the French called *zébrage*), a technique which, like Thayer's method of surface disruption, consisted of painting erratic designs on the surface of a ship, making it visually harder to read through the periscope of a German submarine or U-boat.

When ships were dazzle-painted, they were easy to spot but hard for a torpedo gunner to hit. In the last years of World War I, one-of-a-kind dazzle patterns were applied to thousands of British and American ships, of which fewer than one percent were successfully hit by torpedoes. The US Naval Reserve officer who supervised the dazzle painting of American ships during both World Wars was an artist named Everett Warner from Vinton, Iowa.

From Brest, Fry and Faulkner were sent to Dijon, where they assisted briefly in constructing a "camouflage factory," a 20-acre complex of 40 buildings, including a laboratory, blacksmith shop, machine shop, paint shop, and (for the benefit of the French workers' children) a toy production shop that also was used as a studio for the painters and sculptors.

In addition to manufacturing daily 50,000 square yards of artillery cover (overhanging nets with interwoven canvas strips), the factory also produced disguised observation posts, wooden silhouettes, dummy heads, sniper suits, armor-plated tree trunks and airplane hangar covers.

On February 2, 1918, Fry and Faulkner were transferred to the front lines, where their primary responsibility was the camouflage of artillery positions, to prevent their detection by airplanes. To conceal them, they covered the guns with a camouflage material manufactured at Dijon, made of chicken wire and multi-colored rags.

AT THE BATTLE FRONT, Fry's specialty was camouflaging machine guns and trench mortars. "He had little sense of fear and less of discipline," Faulkner remembered.

He also "had an insatiable curiosity" and "resented taking orders." As a result, he defied regulations and frequently went out exploring alone in abandoned trenches to collect German helmets, belt buckles and other souvenirs.

These forays became his chief interest, and before long he was transferred to Chantilly, where, because he spoke French proficiently, he served as the American liaison to the French camouflage section.

Faulkner and Fry did not meet again until the war ended in late 1918. Both returned to the US, where Fry received several important awards, and continued to take on commissions for statues, fountains and building pediments throughout the country.

Nevertheless, whatever potential he had to become a major American artist was never realized. For the remainder of his long life, he worked out of his studio in Roxbury, Connecticut, where he died in 1966. ■

ROBERT ROSENBLUM *Cubism and Twentieth-Century Art*
The complex, concealed identities of Cubist art found a surprising parallel in the military art of camouflage.

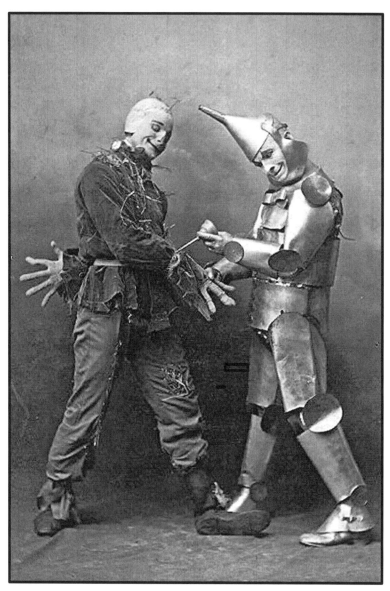

James Samuel Windeatt (1902), photograph of Fred Stone (left) performing as the Scarecrow in the 1902 theatrical version of *The Wizard of Oz,* with David Montgomery in the role of the Tin Woodman. Public domain.

IOWA'S KING OF THE REALM OF THE KOIN

TENNESSEE WILLIAMS *The Glass Menagerie*
...I am the opposite of a stage magician. He gives you an illusion that has the appearance of truth. I give you truth in the pleasant disguise of illusion.

IN 1897, the writer Edna Ferber and her family moved from Ottumwa, Iowa, to Appleton, Wisconsin, where she finished high school.

After graduation, she worked as a reporter for the local newspaper, where she was assigned to interview the magician Harry Houdini, who had grown up in Appleton. Houdini was illusive, but she finally succeeded in speaking to him while the two stood on the street in front of a drugstore, next to a gum and candy machine.

During the interview, Ferber recalled, the two "chatted affably," while Houdini leaned against the candy machine. When they finished talking, he dropped a cold metal object into Ferber's hand. "There's the padlock [to the candy machine,]" he said. "Better give it to the drugstore man. Somebody'll steal all his chewing gum." Ferber was wowed. As she later recalled, "I hadn't seen so much as a movement of his fingers."

HOUDINI HAD been born in Hungary but ended up in Appleton because his father was the rabbi there. As a stage performer, he adopted his professional name in tribute to Robert-Houdin, the famous French magician.

As his reputation grew, Houdini became well-acquainted

with other prominent magicians, one of whom had also grown up in the Midwest, in the state of Iowa. That magician was Tommy Downs (who Houdini initially met in 1893 at the Chicago Worlds Fair), or—as his name appears on posters—T. Nelson Downs, the so-called King of Koins. Even his gravestone describes him as that.

Tommy Downs' hometown is Marshalltown, Iowa, a city whose other claim to celebrity is that it is the birthplace of the film actress Jean Seeberg, who, at age 18, was chosen to star in the film *Saint Joan*.

IF YOU VISIT the town today, it is imperative to tour the Marshall County Historical Society, at the corner of 5th Street and West Main.

They have there a cache of collectibles that pertain to T. Nelson Downs, notably including a strangely elaborate rocking chair (East Indian from Victorian times), which museum guides refer to as "Houdini's wife's rocking chair."

While the origin of that title is unclear, it is said that Houdini's widow (Wilhelmina, known as Bess), whenever she came to visit, insisted on having first choice of that chair. Downs was older than Houdini by several years. And presumably he was taller as well, since Houdini was only 5 feet 5 inches, while his wife Bess was 4 feet 11 (she would fit snuggly in that chair).

Downs' fascination with sleight of hand began when he first saw a magician perform at age twelve. Four years later, his interest had intensified by the time he was hired as a night-shift clerk and telegrapher at the local railway station.

When idle at the telegraph key, he practiced magic using coins and cards. Otherwise, when things were slow, he strolled out to the waiting room and demonstrated his sleight of hand to those who were waiting for trains.

On one occasion, among the passengers who watched his tricks, was Fred Stone of the Stone Brothers, a circus acrobat and actor who would later play the Scarecrow in the 1902 stage version of *The Wizard of Oz*.

More than a dozen years later, by which time Downs was famous, Stone was performing in London, when someone told him he should see an amazing coin magician at the London Palace Theatre. "Well, however good this guy is," Stone replied, "he surely can't be better than a young man I saw years ago at a train station in Marshalltown, Iowa." And yes, it turned out that both performers were Tommy Downs.

T. Nelson Downs (right) with Harry Houdini (second from right) and other magicians. Public domain.

IT WAS DOWNS' astonishing skill at coin manipulation that, obviously, earned him the label of the undisputed King of Koins. Among his best-known coin routines was the *Miser's Dream*.

In that act, as described by another magician, coin after coin was "picked out of the air, from various parts of the performer's body, from the whiskers of some spectator, from a lady's coat" or they might "fall in a shower when someone sneezed." At the peak of his career, he could palm as many as sixty coins.

Not only did he perform at the Palace Theatre in London (one time for 26 consecutive weeks). He was so popular and so well-known internationally that he ended up performing, on an all but continuous schedule, from 1899 through 1912 on the world's most sought-after stages, not just in New York and London, but also at the Folies Bergère in Paris, the Wintergarten in Berlin, and so on.

He performed for royalty as well, including Queen Victoria, her son the Prince of Wales (who would later become king), Czar Nicholas of Russia, Kaiser Wilhelm of Germany, and Emperor Franz Joseph of Austria.

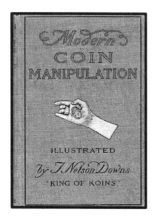 

T. Nelson Downs book and palming coin. Public domain.

BY 1912, at age 42, having earned what today is equivalent to more than a million dollars, Downs retired from the stage, and returned to live in Marshalltown. But he did not retire from performing. He bought a theatre on Main Street, where he himself sometimes performed, and opened a combined stage and motion picture theatre in the same area.

He also sold magic equipment by mail order, as well as the books he had written, and continued to participate in the Society of American Magicians. But his efforts were eventually slowed, by the effects of an illness that started around 1935 (some say diabetes), and of course by the business disasters that came with the Depression.

As Karl Johnson later observed (in *The Magician and the Cardsharp*), Tommy Downs "had dazzled thousands around the world with his *Miser's Dream*, pulling a seemingly endless supply of coins out of the air. But now in the Depression, audiences were longing for *Pennies From Heaven*. Downs was retired, and friends were sending him postage stamps in their letters to be sure he could afford to write back."

His health was worsened by a stroke. He died in 1938, and was buried in Riverside Cemetery in Marshalltown, where some people leave coins on his tombstone.

I MUST SHARE one additional curious detail about Tommy Downs' connection to Iowa. In his life, he married twice, first in 1890. But his wife died following childbirth in 1895, and he remarried ten years later.

What is especially interesting is that his first wife was a woman from Marshalltown named Nellie Stone. She was the daughter of a Canadian immigrant and restaurant owner named Esbon Weed Stone.

Stone and his family had founded Stone's Restaurant, a nationally known Marshalltown dining place, a literal family restaurant, which, while I was growing up, was located under the Third Street Viaduct.

One of its specialities was "Mile High Lemon Chiffon Pie." It was featured in *Life*, *Saturday Evening Post*, and *National Geographic*, and was praised by cookbook guru Duncan Hines. It's location was somewhat out of the way. With no GPS back then, travelers on the Lincoln Highway were told they could find it "Under the Viaduct, by the Vinegar Works." ■

PHYLLIS ROSE *Parallel Lives*
[Charles Dickens] turned watches into tea caddies, made pieces of money fly through the air, burned up pocket watches without burning them. He caused a tiny doll to disappear and then to reappear with little messages and pieces of news for different children in the audience. But his greatest trick, the climax of it all, was his manufacture from an ordinary gentleman's hat of a plum pudding.

Undated detail of a snapshot of the entrance gate to the Gardner family homestead in Spirit Lake, Iowa, site of the infamous attack in 1857. Public domain.

SOPHIE TUCKER
MEETS SPIRIT LAKE

EVELYN WAUGH Decline and Fall III
**I came to the conclusion many years ago that almost all crime is
due to the repressed desire for esthetic expression.**

IN 1961, the American writer Mackinlay Kantor (1904-1977) published a book about Iowa history called *Spirit Lake*. At nearly one thousand pages, it feels gargantuan in length. It took years to research and no doubt equal effort to write. Given its narrative intricacy, some people find it a challenge to read.

Kantor was born in 1904, and grew up in Webster City, Iowa, about 130 miles southeast of Lake Okoboji and the city of Spirit Lake. As a child, he (like most of us) was told the story of what is commonly known as the Spirit Lake Massacre.

In 1857, sparsely situated homes of Euro-American settlers were attacked by Native Americans (Santee Sioux in origin). At least thirty-five area settlers were killed and four women were taken as captives.

Over the years, the inherited oral account of what happened was inevitably one-sided, and one of the goals of Kantor's book was to retell it in a balanced way, albeit in slow and exhaustive detail.

Kantor's book on Spirit Lake was a massive undertaking, with a word count even longer than his earlier, widely-praised novel about Andersonville, the notorious wartime prison camp in southwestern Georgia, where thousands of Union prisoners died during the Civil War. That earlier book, titled *Andersonville*, was initially published in 1955, and was awarded the Pulitzer Prize for Fiction.

ABOUT HALFWAY as the crow flies between Kantor's hometown of Webster City and the site of Spirit Lake is yet another Iowa community, named Algona (from the indigenous term for Algonquin).

At the close of the 19th century, it was one of the railway stops for the legendary "orphan trains," and would later become the location of a camp for World War II German POWs.

Another Algona distinction is its Henry Adams Building, at the corner of East and Moore Streets, a modest brick "architectural gem" designed by Louis Sullivan, the primary mentor of Frank Lloyd Wright.

Iowa artist Gary Kelley (who now resides in Cedar Falls) was born and raised in Algona. In recent years, having grown up hearing about the Spirit Lake Massacre, he took on the challenge of producing an updated version of that historic event in the form of a graphic novel, titled *Moon of the Snowblind: Spirit Lake Massacre* (Ice Cube Press, 2021).

Like Kantor's original epic, Kelley's book is an astonishing effort, although it must have felt at times like a feat of reverse engineering: Unlike Kantor's boundless text of 950 pages, Kelley conveys the same story in fewer than 200 pages.

And since his book is made up of a sequence of cartoon-style panels, there may be only a handful of words (in traditional "word balloons") on any one page. His exacting terseness makes it work (it will undoubtedly reach a wider and far younger audience), and Kelley's account may have an impact equivalent to, if different from, the earlier effort of Kantor.

I FIRST read *Spirit Lake* about fifty years ago. Kelly's graphic novel led me back to Kantor himself. I was completely unaware of how convoluted was Kantor's life, both in his youthful Webster City days, and in his later difficult years as a famous author.

For example, I was unaware of his candid account about growing up in Iowa, titled *But Look, the Morn* (1939).

That memoir was at times disturbing to read, but it helped to mitigate the shock of more detailed episodes in two other books about him: one, a memoir by his son, Tim Kantor, titled *My Father's Voice* (1988), and a second memoir by his grandson, Tom Schroder, *The Most Famous Writer Who Ever Lived* (2016).

Portrait photograph of American novelist Mackinlay Kantor, c1950. Public domain. Wikimedia Commons.

In all three of those books, I was surprised to learn about Kantor's father's criminal past. As might be surmised from their family name, Kantor's paternal ancestry was Jewish, and among his long line of ancestors were Talmudic scholars, cantors, and rabbis. His father was John Martin Kantor, who had been born in Sweden in 1878, emigrated to the US as a teenager, and grew up in Chicago.

At some point, around 1894, when John Kantor was about fifteen, he had a change of religious belief, and converted from Judaism to Christianity.

A few years later, he joined a traveling evangelists' troupe, and toured the Midwest as a featured speaker, bearing witness to his new-found life as a "converted Jew."

Among the places where he spoke was a small Iowa town, where he was befriended by a wealthy farmer, who decided he should lend support. That person provided the funding for John Kantor to enroll at Drake Bible College (which later became Drake University) in Des Moines.

Gary Kelley, cover illustration and design for *Moon of the Snowblind: Spirit Lake*, Ice Cube Press.

WHILE AT DRAKE Kantor met another student, a young, beautiful woman from Webster City named Virginia McKinlay (called Effie). They fell in love, married in November 1899, and, one year later, had a child.

After serving at several posts, John Kantor's pastoral options collapsed when it became evident that he had repeatedly been duplicitous—he had not graduated from Drake, nor had he ever been ordained.

Beset by this and other concerns, he fled from Iowa around 1903, abandoning his pregnant wife to await the birth of their second child, a son who was actually christened as Benjamin McKinlay Kantor, a name that he would later replace with MacKinlay Kantor, who was known by friends as "Mack."

With the aid of online sources, it is now possible to retrace the life of MacKinlay Kantor's father, but the full story would likely be as long as one of his son's famous novels.

To shorten a (very) long story, Kantor's errant father had renewed but very infrequent contact with his first wife and their

Chicago-based showgirl and performer Sophie Tucker, known as "The Last of the Red-Hot Mamas," c1910. Public domain.

children. Instead, he moved to Chicago at the height of the Prohibition era, married a second time, and appears to have had a relationship with the showgirl Sophie Tucker, "The Last of the Red-Hot Mamas."

Over the years, he was "in and out" of prison—*in* because of various crimes, *out* with the help of influential friends (both criminal and otherwise) in Chicago's high places, most notably its infamous mayor, William "Big Bill" Thompson.

As he neared the age of sixty, John Kantor was convicted of involvement in a notorious stock fraud scandal, and ended up serving twenty months at the Sing Sing Correctional Facility in Ossining, New York.

He died in 1956 in New York.

JOHN KANTOR appears to have led the life of a swindler and a con man. He was despised by his wife and his son.

But judgements are shaped by comparative means: Behavior is "good" in relation to "bad," and "honesty" becomes defined in contrast to its opposite. In reading the various sources about the life of MacKinlay Kantor (the famous son), it soon becomes apparent that he himself had qualities that were short of sanctimonious.

Roy R. Behrens (2007), poster for holocaust program series, College of Humanities and Fine Arts, University of Northern Iowa (2007).

The accounts of his own son and his nephew portray a gifted writer who was tormented and complex. Throughout his adult life, Kantor the novelist struggled with intense, constant proclivities toward alcohol, extra-marital affairs, and other familiar afflictions.

For readers who, for many years, have unquestionably admired the achievements of Kantor as an author, these darker aspects of his life are distressing to be told about.

There is so much to process in coming to understand Kantor's life. Looking back on what I learned, one moment sharply stands apart: Near the end of WWII, Kantor was serving in Europe as an American war correspondent. Embedded with the US Army in Germany, he arrived at Buchenwald, the dreadful concentration camp, in April 1945, one day after its liberation by the Allies.

Twelve days later, he wrote a letter to his wife, Irene, attempting to convey the horror of what he had recently witnessed. That letter has survived and is quoted in the memoir by the couple's son. While its content is disturbing, it does not begin to compare with the shock of having been present.

SHORTLY AFTER the end of WWII, Kantor embarked on writing *Andersonville*, for which he won the Pulitzer Prize. During the American Civil War, Andersonville had been a camp for Union POWs, where 13,000 prisoners died from malnutrition, scurvy, diarrhea, and dysentery.

In side by side comparisons of photographs of starving inmates in German concentration camps and the barely-surviving prisoners at Andersonville, the resemblance is all too disturbing—especially at a moment when the world is once again at war, and non-combatant fatalities and other atrocities are as commonplace as ever. ■

American History Puzzle Picture

An American camouflaged transport ship leaving New York on its way across the Atlantic with our American soldiers. Find a sailor.

Clemens Gretter (c1928), syndicated newspaper picture puzzle. In this reference to WWI dazzle-camouflaged ships, the lost sailor has apparently fallen overboard, and is floating in the water below the ship. Public domain.

RIPLEY'S GHOST
BELIEVE IT OR NOT

GEORGE BERNARD SHAW
Life isn't about finding yourself. Life is
about creating yourself.

CLEMENS GRETTER was the (unheralded) artist who drew the newspaper cartoons for Robert Ripley's *Believe It or Not*. He did lots of other things as well.

It might even be said that he left a large footprint during his lifetime. And yet, he is a challenge to track, partly because, when signing his work, he used so many different names.

When he was born, he was Joseph Clemens Gretter. As a "ghost artist," he was not allowed to sign his name to the *Believe It or Not* cartoons, since Ripley took sole credit for those. But when his other illustrations were published, they were variously credited to J. Clemens Gretter, Clemens J. Gretter, Clemens Gretter, Clem Gretter, Clem Gretta, Clem, and Gretta.

GRETTER WAS an Iowan at heart, but he wasn't born in Iowa. He was born in Earl Park, Indiana (just south of Chicago, near Lafayette), in 1904, the first-born of ten offspring of dirt-poor Catholic farmers.

His family led a daunting life. When he was a child, they left Indiana and moved to Nampa, Idaho, where Gretter first attended school. At some point the family moved back to the Midwest, and settled on a farm near Crookston, Minnesota.

In 1918, when Clem was fourteen, they traded that property

for a farm of equivalent size in south central Iowa, near Avery, which is on the railroad line. It is six miles from the mining community of Albia, and twenty miles west of Ottumwa.

The ensuing years were important for him, and, in later life, he considered himself an Iowan. Some published accounts mistakenly claim that he was born in Iowa.

While still in middle school, Gretter was an altar boy at the Catholic Church in Albia, and admired the parish priest. When that priest was reassigned to Davenport, Gretter expressed interest in going with him, with the intent of beginning to study for the priesthood. His parents objected, and Gretter instead entered high school in Avery.

THE DAY THAT his parents refused his request was both traumatic and pivotal, as he would later describe in a strangely confessional memoir about dream interpretation.

He recalls that, in response to their refusal, he felt terribly dejected. He left the house in protest, and walked out to a creek on the farm. There, he walked by a site on the creek bed where there was a familiar deposit of white clay.

Sitting down, he began to wedge and shape the clay. He soon became preoccupied, and completely forgot about the disagreement with his parents. Instead, he grew increasingly interested in the process of working with clay.

Always responsible for farm chores, he had never before been permitted to engage in such useless activities as making clay sculptures. He became all but ecstatic when he found that he was able to make the likeness of a human face (it was a bust of Socrates).

It was late afternoon when he gathered up his "artwork," and ran back to the house to proudly show his parents. In his memoir, he recalls that as he neared the house, he was met by his mother, who had been frantically searching for him. She said, "Where in the world have you been, we've been looking for you all afternoon." And then, looking down at his sculpture, she said,

"And where did you find that?"

"Breathless with excitement," he recalled, "I exclaimed, 'I made it, mom. I made it!'" He had been "called"—but not to the priesthood. That afternoon, he knew that he was going to be an artist.

SOON AFTER Gretter entered high school, and apparently had a glorious time, since, for years, he spoke of it glowingly in news interviews, as well as in his memoir.

While attending Avery High School, he wrote, "[I] fell in love with my teacher, and by the time I graduated, every room in the school was decorated with one or more of my statuary." In his memoir, he published a photograph of her, as well as a postcard she sent him twenty years earlier.

Also in his memoir is a photograph of what is described as "the author's first sculpture" (except for Socrates), a bust of US President Warren G. Harding, which was described when on display as having been "carved by a local farm boy with his cornhusking peg."

It was made of that white Monroe County clay, and had never been kiln-fired. It was impermanent as a result, and when Gretter and his wife returned to visit his Iowa hometown in 1958, he found that all his sculptures had fallen apart, or had been dropped and shattered.

FOLLOWING HIS completion of high school, when Gretter's family lost their farm, they moved to Indiana, where his parents were both originally from.

At age nineteen, he moved to Chicago, where he took art courses at night at the Art Institute of Chicago, while working as a bus boy and clothing salesman during the day. He was subsequently hired by the *Chicago Tribune* as an illustrator and cartoonist, for which he made hidden figure cartoons called *Hippity Skip Puzzles*.

In time, Gretter became adept not at sculpture, but at

American History Puzzle Picture

Stonewall Jackson and Barbara Fritchie. When she appeared at a window waving a Union flag, Jackson said, "Who touches but a hair on yon' gray head, dies like a dog, march on." Find a Union soldier.

Another of Clemens Gretter's early syndicated newspaper picture puzzles (1928). The caption instructs the reader to "find a Union soldier." Hint: He's upside down and forms part of the tree in the center. Public domain.

drawing and painting, the two skills that enabled him to move to New York City during the Depression, and to pursue a successful, productive career as a designer and illustrator.

Gretter was prolific. He illustrated magazine stories, and provided illustrations for serial novels (such as *The Hardy Boys*), newspapers, and comic books (including *Weird Tales* and *Fun Comics*). As a syndicated newspaper cartoonist, he continued to produce "picture puzzles," in which he hid figures that readers were challenged to locate.

His claim to fame (of sorts) began in 1941, when he "ghosted" as the artist for the syndicated newspaper feature, *Ripley's Believe It or Not*, which continued for eight years until Robert Ripley died.

Soon after, Gretter and his wife moved to southwestern Connecticut, where they raised four children, while he continued to work in Manhattan. He died in 1988.

SO FAR, SO good. Or not so good if you read his memoir, *Chain of Reasoning* (1978). In that book, he claims that in 1964, a system for "deciphering dreams" was revealed to him in a ten-volume set of encyclopedias (published in 1899) that he bought used at a furniture store.

It enabled him to unravel arcane encrypted secrets about the universe, none of which I have been able to parse. So compelling were these revelations to him that he began to send registered letters to Dwight Eisenhower, Pope John XXII, Nikita Khrushchev, and Lyndon Johnson, which are included in his book, along with their courteous, if cautious, replies.

To confirm Gretter's insights, his loyal wife accompanied him on a non-stop cross-continental tour of the Canadian Shield. And in 1975, in advance of the US Bicentennial, he petitioned the city council where he lived to sanction his proposal to build two "antipodal cairns" (ten-foot pyramids), one in Connecticut (which was actually constructed) and the other on an island near Tasmania, directly opposite on the globe.

That's all I know—believe it or not. ■

Unidentified civilian painters, during WWI, applying various colors to the sides of a dazzle-camouflaged ship. These areas were first marked off with chalk, and labeled with names of the colors. Public domain.

OTTUMWA'S THEATRICAL
SHIP CAMOUFLEUR

WALLACE STEVENS
From time immemorial the philosophers and other scene
painters have daubed the sky with dazzle paint.

AMERICAN NOVELIST Edna Ferber, who was originally from Kalamazoo, Michigan, moved with her family to Ottumwa, Iowa, in 1890, where they lived for seven years.

She was five years old at the time, and her Jewish father was a shopkeeper. With a population then of 14,000, Ottumwa was a rough coal-mining town.

Years later, describing her childhood, Ferber recalled that, while walking home one evening, she turned a corner and witnessed a lynching.

She also clearly remembered anti-Semitic incidents, such as the gauntlet of verbal abuse by onlookers on the street as she delivered his lunch to her father.

FERBER WAS undoubtedly acquainted with another Jewish child, a boy of the same age, who also lived in Ottumwa then. His name was Carol Mayer Sax. His father, a prosperous downtown merchant named Jacob Sax, had immigrated from Germany. He owned Ottumwa's finest clothing store, among the largest in the state.

Wealthy and civic-minded, Carol's parents were well-known for their charitable activities. They lived in an opulent residence in what is now known as the Fifth Street Historic District.

After their parents died in the 1920s, Carol Sax and his sister (both of whom had left Iowa years earlier) made an effort to preserve the family's mansion "as a virtual museum and memorial to their parents who had filled the home with art treasures, collections of antiques, and rare furnishings."

The garden on its grounds was known as "one of the city's showplaces." But in 1945, the property was donated to the church next door, and at some point the house was dismantled.

LIKE FERBER, Carol Sax was destined to have a career in the arts, albeit not nearly as famous as hers. Sax was not a writer, but he would become modestly prominent as an artist and designer in Baltimore and New York (where he designed costumes and theatre sets), and as a teacher of art and design at the Maryland Institute of Art and Design, and the University of Kentucky.

As a co-founder of the Vagabond Theatre in Baltimore, he was an early participant in the Little Theatre Movement (as were Jig Cook and Susan Glaspel from Davenport). And, oddly enough—but, actually, not so odd at all—he was also briefly notable for his involvement in ship camouflage. During World War I, partly because of his expertise in scenic design (which uses perspective distortions), Sax worked as a camouflage artist (called a "camoufleur") for the US Shipping Board.

BUT BEFORE ALL that, having finished high school, he left Ottumwa and enrolled not at a university (where studio art was not yet taught) but at the Art Institute of Chicago. As was customary, he then went on to study at the Art Students League in New York, and the National Academy of Design.

He also attended Columbia University, presumably to learn to teach. If so, he certainly knew, and possibly was a student of a Columbia artist-educator named Alon Bement. Georgia O'Keeffe had also been a student there, and Bement, according to her, was a major influence when he and Arthur Wesley Dow were her teachers. Like Sax, Bement also served as a wartime camoufleur, applying camouflage schemes to ships.

THE WAR ENDED in November 1918, and soon after Carol Sax returned home to visit. He was interviewed in Ottumwa by the *Des Moines Register*, which featured a story about him on February 2, 1919, with the headline IOWAN AIDED US AS CAMOUFLEUR.

Two examples of WWI American dazzle-camouflaged ships. At the top is the USS *West Galoc* (1918), and below that is the USS *Crawl Keys* (1918). The opposite sides (not shown) were entirely different designs. Public domain.

He talked about his civilian wartime duties, which involved developing camouflage patterns for American merchant ships, to guard against encounters with German submarines (called U-boats).

However, these were bewildering camouflage schemes. Unlike ground camouflage, they were not attempts to make a ship invisible, since any vessel was readily detected by the smoke from its stacks, as well as the sounds of its motors.

Instead, this kind of camouflage (known as "dazzle" at the time) was designed to distort the ship's appearance, as viewed from a distance through a submarine periscope, and to subvert the calculations of the torpedo gunner. In other words, the primary effect of ship camouflage was not to make it hard to see, but to make it hard to hit.

Dazzle camouflaged ships were inevitably lampooned, and described in news stories as "cubist nightmares," "sea-going easter eggs," "a Russian toyshop gone mad," and even as the delirium tremens.

WWI American ship, the USS *W.L. Steed*, in dazzle camouflage (1918). Public domain.

FOLLOWING WWI, Sax returned to teaching at the Maryland Institute of Art. But in 1921, he moved to Lexington, Kentucky, where he served for eight years as Head of the Art Department at the University of Kentucky.

There, he founded the Romany Theatre, a "little theatre" that was initially housed inside an abandoned building on the edge of the campus.

The building's exterior was so dismal that Sax and students came up with a promotional ploy of inviting students, townspeople, and passers-by to a "painting party" for the purpose of enlivening the building's drab appearance. When the party ended, the building was "adorned with gaily colored splotches of paint, campus caricatures, and football scores…"

Some people said it reminded them of WWI dazzle ship camouflage, and a magazine described it as "a nightmare, a riot of color, resembling nothing so much as the palette of an artist with delirium tremens."

CAROL SAX left Kentucky in 1929 to work as a theatre designer in New York. For the remaining decades of his life, he focused on stage productions and motion pictures, including three brief interludes: one in Paris, in which he tried (unsuccessfully) to acclimate French audiences to American plays; another in Manchester, England, as managing producer of its repertory theatre; and in Hollywood, where he was the assistant to film director Alan Crossman (director of *The Jazz Singer*, the first significant "talkie").

Infrequently, he would return to Ottumwa, to encourage art exhibitions and award scholarships.

What may have been his last visit took place in October 1941, when he spoke about "Art and the Theatre" (which turned into a discussion about abstract art) at the community's art center. Twenty years later, he died in New York at age 76. ■

ANON *Our Futurist Shipping*
…the camouflage artist has painted our vessels with bizarre designs in all colors of the rainbow…a steamship no longer resembles a steamship. It looks like a futurist nightmare.

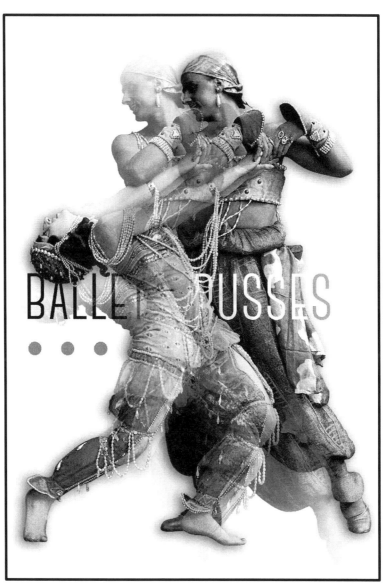

Roy R. Behrens, from a series of posters about the Russian Ballet (2023).

THE IMPRESARIO
OF BOOK DESIGN

JAY SATTERFIELD
He [Merle Armitage] was highbrow and lowbrow while
selling "culture" to a middlebrow audience.

IN THE EARLY 1940s, shortly after the writer Henry Miller had returned from Paris, he concluded that a noncommercial artist in America "has as much chance for survival as a sewer rat."

Refusing to borrow or to hire out for "stultifying work," he sent out a letter inviting support from the readers of *The New Republic*, requesting, among other things, "old clothes, shirts, socks, etc. I am 5 feet 8 inches tall, weigh 150 pounds, 15 1/2 neck, 38 chest, 32 waist, hat and shoes both size 7 to 7 1/2. Love corduroys."

The appeal worked and a number of curious mailings arrived, one of which contained a complete tuxedo. "What'll I ever do with this?" Miller asked a friend, then used it to dress up a scarecrow that sat for a generation on the picket fence in front of his Partington Ridge house in Big Sur, California.

AMONG THE OTHER gifts was a cash contribution from Merle Armitage, who was an Iowa-born book designer, civil engineer, set designer, concert promoter, gourmet, art collector, and author. Armitage was also living in California, and soon after, when he visited Miller's home for the first time, he described his own profession as that of an "impresario."

"But I have heard that you were a writer?" replied Miller.

"If the truth were known," Armitage explained, "I write books so that I will be able to design them."

In fact, by that time Armitage had designed nearly two dozen books, some of which he had also written.

But Miller was incredulous: "Does a book have to be *designed*?" he asked. "A book is a book, and I don't see how you can do much about it."

BORN IN 1893 on a farm in the vicinity of Mason City, Iowa, Armitage's lifelong interest in graphic design, engineering and problem-solving can be traced back to his childhood.

His paternal grandfather had been a friend of J.I. Case, an important pioneer in the development of steam-driven farm machinery; while a few miles east of the Armitage home was Charles City, site of the invention of the first gasoline-powered farm tractor.

One day as the young Armitage and his father were helping a neighboring farmer named Wright with the repair of a windmill, a messenger rode up on horseback and handed the man a telegram. "He passed it around," Armitage remembered, "and my father read it aloud. It said: We flew today at Kitty Hawk, and it was signed Orville and Wilbur."

Armitage was as much impressed by the immediacy of the telegram as by its message: "The two were equally exciting to me: to fly through the air, to send a message over the wire. Both left me absolutely enslaved to things mechanical."

His father, according to Armitage, was a dreamer who should never have become a businessman. Nevertheless, "he had great vision," and, at a time when steers ranged free to feed on grass, he made a fortune (which he later lost in a market crash) on the innovation of corn-fed beef.

"Finding that corn grew luxuriantly in the new land," recalled Armitage, his father "conceived the idea that purchasing range cattle and feeding them all the corn they could eat for two months would produce new flavor."

It was by the influence of his father that he became avidly interested in machines, farm implements, steam locomotives and automobiles, and in engineering and inventing.

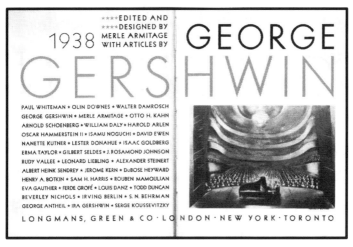

****EDITED AND
****DESIGNED BY
1938 MERLE ARMITAGE
WITH ARTICLES BY

GEORGE

GERSHWIN

PAUL WHITEMAN • OLIN DOWNES • WALTER DAMROSCH
GEORGE GERSHWIN • MERLE ARMITAGE • OTTO H. KAHN
ARNOLD SCHOENBERG • WILLIAM DALY • HAROLD ARLEN
OSCAR HAMMERSTEIN II • ISAMU NOGUCHI • DAVID EWEN
NANETTE KUTNER • LESTER DONAHUE • ISAAC GOLDBERG
ERMA TAYLOR • GILBERT SELDES • J. ROSAMOND JOHNSON
RUDY VALLEE • LEONARD LIEBLING • ALEXANDER STEINERT
ALBERT HEINK SENDREY • JEROME KERN • DuBOSE HEYWARD
HENRY A. BOTKIN • SAM H. HARRIS • ROUBEN MAMOULIAN
EVA GAUTHIER • FERDE GROFÉ • LOUIS DANZ • TODD DUNCAN
BEVERLEY NICHOLS • IRVING BERLIN • S. N. BEHRMAN
GEORGE ANTHEIL • IRA GERSHWIN • SERGE KOUSSEVITZKY

LONGMANS, GREEN & CO · LONDON · NEW YORK · TORONTO

Merle Armitage (1938), title page spread for his book on George Gershwin

At the same time, it was his mother (a school teacher) who encouraged his artistic abilities by the choice of the pictures she hung in their home, by the brazen act of painting the front door a bright red (thus creating "a neighborhood sensation"), and by reinforcing his early attempts at drawing.

His mother's parents, the Jacobs, lived in Mason City, which Armitage described as "a sweet Iowa town of tree-shaded streets and friendly people," the town that was later immortalized as "River City" in *The Music Man* by Meredith Willson. It was also the boyhood home of Bil Baird, the well-known puppeteer.

Today, adjacent to Willson's birthplace is the Charles H. MacNider Museum, a majestic English Tudor Revival mansion that bears the name of an Armitage family friend, who was also the owner of the First National Bank.

When Armitage was still a teenager, it was a rivalry between MacNider and another Mason City banker that resulted in the hiring of a young Chicago-based architect named Frank Lloyd Wright (unrelated to the Wright brothers, apparently) to design a new bank, offices and an adjoining hotel for the City National Bank (which remains and has recently been restored).

Within the next decade, Wright (until he was discredited by eloping with a client's wife), Walter Burley Griffin, William Drummond, and other capable young architects designed innovative Prairie Style houses within a planned community, so that Armitage's little home town is now widely known as the site of a marvelous cluster of gem-like Early Modern homes.

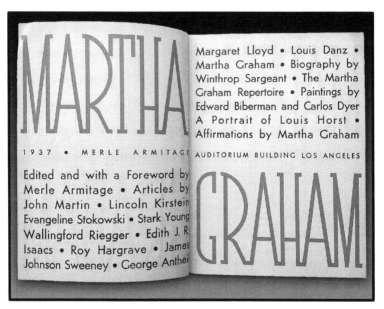

Merle Armitage (1937), title spread for his book on Martha Graham.

THE ANCESTORS OF both Wright and Armitage had settled in Wisconsin, from which the latter had then moved to northern Iowa. Wright was commissioned to design the City National Bank in 1908 through the efforts of J.E. Markeley, a friend and Mason City businessman whose two daughters were students of Wright's aunt at her Hillside School, in Spring Green, Wisconsin, which was housed in buildings that Wright had designed.

By the time the Mason City hotel project began, Armitage was 15 years old, and he and his family had already moved to a cattle ranch near Lawrence, Kansas, and then onto Texas.

In one of his autobiographies, Armitage refers to the architect's son, Frank Lloyd Wright, Jr. (known as Lloyd Wright), as "an old friend." In 1923, when the American press reported, incorrectly, that Wright's Imperial Hotel in Tokyo had been devastated by an earthquake, Armitage (in his capacity as a publicist) was recruited by the architect to help to set the record straight.

They remained what Armitage described as "casual friends" for many years, dining together for the last time in New York in 1953. Wright died in 1959.

ART, DESIGN, ADVERTISING, and mechanical engineering: In Armitage's young imagination, these allied yet differing interests combined in the form of a breathtaking automobile, the Packard.

It was his childhood fascination with this motor vehicle, he recalled in 1945, "[which satisfied] esthetic as well as utilitarian demands," that led him to start a reference archive of Packard advertising material, publications that, like the machine they advertised, "reflected advanced design and a kind of artistic integrity."

Brochures of other makes of that time usually contained retouched half-tone illustrations, hard and unlovely as those in heavy-hardware catalogs. Packard used "distinguished line drawings, excellent typography, and hand lettering which would be acceptable today." He was also influenced by the "sleek and smart" styling of the passenger trains on the Santa Fe Railway (known then as the Kansas City, Mexico and Orient Railroad Company), which he noticed as early as 1902, when he and father drove to Lawrence.

Later, Armitage remembered that "The literature and advertising of the Santa Fe, even its world-renowned symbol (of Aztec origin) suggest discernment, and a sophistication seldom associated with a railroad." Like Packard, here then was an early examplar of making the mundane appear to be fresh.

HAVING NEVER attended college, it was the corporate image and advertising publications of Packard and the Santa Fe Railway, said Armitage, "together with the scant treasures of our library, [that] were in a very personal sense my substitutes for college and university...my first contacts with esthetic appreciation and the cosmopolitan amenities of life."

Given Armitage's childhood influences, it is fitting that his first two jobs (beginning at age 17) were as a civil engineer in Texas, apparently connected with the Santa Fe Railway, and then as a graphic designer in the advertising department of the Packard Motor Car Company in Detroit.

He remained in these positions for less than a year, and soon after decided that he should become a theatre set designer, a move that would lead inadvertently to a lucrative 30-year career as a concert impresario.

ARMITAGE IS MOSTLY remembered today as an extraordinary book designer, who would later also be the art director of *Look* magazine (1949-1954), a serious collector of fine art (Dürer, Rembrandt, Goya, Gauguin, Cézanne, Van Gogh, Picasso, Marin, Klee, and Kandinsky), and a past president of the American Institute of Graphic Arts (1950-1951).

But during the first 50 years of his life (as he explained to Henry Miller), he earned an ample income as the promoter and manager of dancers, opera singers, and opera and ballet companies. Among his illustrious clients were Anna Pavlova, Yvette Guilbert, Feodor Chaliapin, Amelita Galli-Curci, Mary Garden, Rosa Ponselle, and the Ballet Russes.

He was also the co-founder and general manager of the Los Angeles Grand Opera Association, a board member of the Los Angeles Symphony Orchestra, and ably served as the manager of the Philharmonic Auditorium of Los Angeles.

He knew and authored books about some of the finest artists of the century, among them Igor Stravinsky, Martha Graham, George Gershwin, Pablo Picasso, Rockwell Kent, and Edward Weston.

Armitage's success as an impresario, as noted by Jay Satterfield, was due in part to his willingness to promote "highbrow" performances by using "lowbrow" advertising ploys, including false scandals and quasi-erotic suggestion.

At the time, announcements of concerts were usually made quietly through restrained, tasteful notices, in contrast to slapstick, flamboyant affairs like the circus.

Armitage's innovation was to stake out a middle ground: By promoting cultural events in much the same way that automobiles and railways were advertised, he believed that a much wider audience might "be led to realize that the arts, and their enjoyment, were reasonably normal activities... needing to be classified neither with afternoon tea nor epileptic fits."

As time went on, he explained, "I became more and more convinced that posters, advertisements in newspapers and magazines, as well as thousands of announcements and circulars used by a concert manager, must reflect the quality of the performer not only in the text, but more important, in the design. Soon I found myself laying out every piece of printing concerned with my concerts, opera or ballet seasons."

IT WAS THIS same philosophy that prompted him to become a book designer, resulting from his decision to use phenomenal books to promote artists whom he admired; not just concert performers, but visual artists, composers and writers as well.

Determined "to work only with publishers who would give me a free hand in design," he not only often wrote or edited his own books, in many cases he was also the publisher.

Of the more than two dozen volumes that Armitage both authored and designed are *Rockwell Kent* (Knopf, 1932), *George Gershwin* (Longmans, 1938), *So-Called Modern Art* (Weyhe,

1939), *United States Navy* (Longmans, 1940), *Notes on Modern Printing* (Rudge, 1945), *Rendezvous with the Book* (McKibbin, 1949), *Railroads of America* (Little Brown 1952), and two autobiographies, *Accent on America* (Weyhe, 1939) and *Accent on Life* (Iowa State University Press, 1965).

In addition, he designed more than 40 other books which he either edited or wrote essays for, and over 60 others by other authors.

In the books of his own writings (his autobiographies, for example, or those in which he talks about the design of books), portions of the narrative are often recycled, if somewhat revised and reshuffled, so that their enduring significance is more as experiments in book design than as freshly written texts.

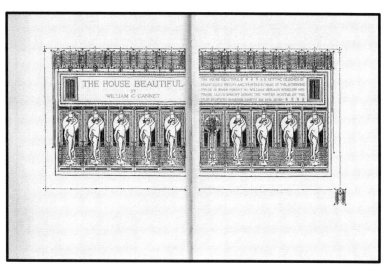

Frank Lloyd Wright (1897), title spread for *The House Beautiful*.

WHEN ARMITAGE WAS four years old, Frank Lloyd Wright had collaborated with one of his own clients on an "artist's book" about esthetics, the soul, and domestic architecture, titled *The House Beautiful* (Auvergne Press, 1897).

The text was derived from a popular talk by a nationally-known Unitarian minister, William C. Gannett. Wright designed the book, while his client, William H. Winslow, set the type and hand-printed an edition of 90 copies in the basement of his new home, only 20 of which now survive.

Thirty-five years later, Wright wrote and designed a second extraordinary volume, titled *An Autobiography*. The first edition was published in 1932 by Longmans, Green and Company, based in London and New York; the second, which came out in 1943, by Duell, Sloan and Pearce in New York. Both editions are much sought after by admirers of book design, largely because of the boldness with which Wright treats the section openings as continuous spreads, not just single facing fields that happen to be juxtaposed.

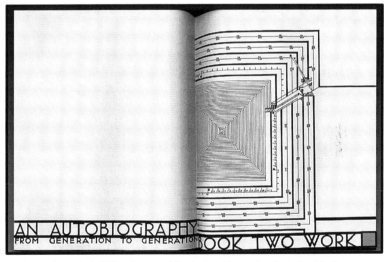

Frank Lloyd Wright (1932), title spread for *An Autobiography: Book Two Work*.

Perhaps the most stirring example is the magnificent title spread for *Book Two Work*. Wright approached book design with the same "organic form" approach that governed his architecture, with the result, as a critic declared at the time, that the design of his autobiography "compares in brilliance and originality with his buildings."

AS RICHARD HENDEL insightfully stated in *On Book Design*, "Designers are to books what architects are to buildings." Merle Armitage designed his first book in 1929, and in subsequent years, he designed at least 9 books for Longmans, and 13 for Duell, Sloan and Pearce (including several of his best known titles), the publishers who were responsible for Wright's autobiography.

In light of their contacts, one wonders to what degree Armitage, the *enfant terrible* of book design, was inspired by the work of Wright, the bad boy of architecture, and vice versa.

While Armitage admired Wright's architecture, he also liked to make it known that "on the prairies, and long before Frank Lloyd Wright became an influence, the Santa Fe [Railway] had constructed its stations on a horizontal motif."

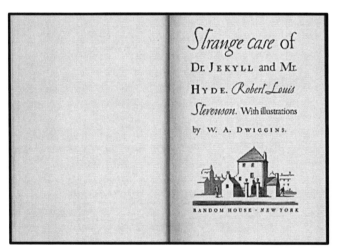

W.A. Dwiggins (1929), title spread for *Strange Case of Dr. Jekyll and Mr. Hyde.*

One wonders too to what extent Wright and Armitage were influenced by W.A. Dwiggins' *Layout in Advertising* (1928) or that designer's celebrated interpretations of Robert Louis Stevenson's *The Strange Case of Dr. Jeckyll and Mr. Hyde* (Knopf, 1929) and H.G. Wells' *The Time Machine* (Random House, 1931).

Anyone who cared about book design in those days, wrote Armitage, "was aware of the Nonesuch and the Golden Cockerel Presses as well as the work of Eric Gill, Francis Meynell, Stanley Morison, and others in England."

He himself collected the books of Bruce Rogers ("perhaps the greatest designer of them all") and "had long admired the distinguished work of such Americans as W.A. Dwiggins, with its Oriental influence."

In Dwiggins' layout for *The Power of Print-and Men* (Mergenthaler, 1936), there is a geometric sweep and use of the tactics that Armitage called "my inventions" that "stirred violent criticism" and caused him, in certain circles, to be reviled as "the destroyer of book tradition, the bad boy of typography, the usurper of the placid pools of bookmaking": "i.e., use of the end sheets, double-page title pages, large readable type, generous margins, etc."

Other notable aspects of Armitage's books, as Hendel has noted, are "his 'cinematic' treatment of the opening pages" and his "exuberant typography."

ARMITAGE WAS just as direct and outspoken as Wright, and if he was despised or avoided (George Macy called him "that bull-in-our-china-shop"), it surely was partly because of the tone with which he communicated.

He was, as described by a close friend, Robert M. Purcell, "a mercurial man in the truest sense. He was like quicksilver, and no thumb could hold him down. He was quick to joy, quick to anger, quick to create. He, like most of us, liked appreciation of what he did, and was quick to take umbrage if he was crossed, although he was a good resounding arguer and would take his lumps if he lost a point, or bellow with laughter when he won."

In photographs, Armitage is a big man with a huge head and broad smile, who often wore a cowboy hat and string tie, a person who would not be popular now in an age of political correctness and disingenuous double-talk.

According to Purcell, "He had a mammoth lust for food, and the build to prove it; he liked hearty food, no nincompoop lemon jello salad with shreds of lettuce for him. He lusted after art, art that dominated and spoke out, no pastels and chalk for him. A lust for good music, not a tinkling piano and Chaminade, but Wagner, Brahms, Beethoven, Bach, and among the neo-moderns, Satie, Ravel, and Stravinsky. A lust for good conversation, and in no way detouring away from a hearty argument with rolling thunderous opinions."

He was literally lusty as well. He used up four marriages, the last one ending sadly in an annulment, lasting no more than two months.

A few years later, when Armitage was close to 80 years old and living alone on his Manzanita Ranch near Yucca Valley, California, his friend Purcell "happened to comment on having seen him with a very nice looking widow of about forty, four decades his junior."

"He said, 'Oh, yes. She comes out to the ranch and services me.' I had never heard that term in that context. It came probably from his Iowa farm youth where his father 'covered' cows in order to breed tremendous herds and became one of the first major 'feeders' in Iowa, where feeding now is a bigger business than breeding."

FRANK LLOYD WRIGHT was, in contrast, short and slim. It must have been more than amusing to see the huge figure of Armitage, looking even larger by comparison, at the feet of the elephantine ego that lived in the undersized physical temple of the self-described "world's greatest architect."

At their last luncheon together, Wright complained to Armitage that some people believed that his school at Taliesin West produced only "little Frank Lloyd Wrights." "But just remember this, young man," he said to Armitage, "there are no little Frank Lloyd Wrights."

Nor was there anything puny about Merle Armitage. His was

a boisterous ego that lived in a spacious body, a bombastic tree of a figure that fell from a fatal stroke on March 15, 1975.

Years earlier, the always impish Wright poked fun at the expansiveness of Armitage, both physical and social, when he gave him a signed photograph of himself by Yosef Karsh: It is inscribed "To Merle, the Armitage" and dated February 30. It's a day of course that doesn't exist. ■

CARL SANDBURG *Always the Young Strangers*
Early the mother pronounced it "Sholly," which later became "Sharlie" and still later the correct "Charlie," while the Old Man stuck to "Sholly, do dis" and "Sholly, do dat." She learned to pronounce "is" as "iz'' and "has" as "haz" while with him it stayed "iss" and "hass." He said "de" for "the," "wenlup" for "envelope," "Hotty do" for "How do you do?," "yelly clay" for "yellow clay," "rellroad" for "railroad," "Gilsburg" for "Galesburg," "Sveden" for Sweden," "helty" for "healthy." ... Anyone who couldn't get what he was saying was either dumb or not listening. He invented a phrase of his own for scolding Mart and me. When he said, "Du strubbel," we knew he meant "You stupid" and he was probably correct. He would impress us about a scheme he believed impossible to work out, "You could not do dat if you wass de Czar of all de Russias."

BUDD SCHULBERG about Hollywood film producer Louis B. Mayer
He was the Czar of the all the rushes.

Anon, portrait photograph of Charles W. Williams, horse racing celebrity from Independence, Iowa (c1895). Public domain.

HORSE RACING'S
ONE-TIME POOH-BAH

WILL ROGERS
A difference of opinion is what makes horse
racing and missionaries.

IN AN ISSUE OF *The New York Times* on February 20, 1899, there was a curious article on an unexpected visitor at a horse sale in that city. The visitor, from Galesburg, Illinois, was Charles W. Williams.

He was recognized by reporters as a former celebrity in the world of horse racing. It seems he had once been the owner of a world-famous trotting horse, a sire named Axtell, who had set a world record at Independence, Iowa, on Williams' kite-shaped racetrack.

But that had been almost a decade before, and Williams' luck had plummeted. Indeed, those who spoke to Williams that day were surprised by how poorly he was dressed. He "looked like 30 cents," one person remarked.

He was attired in a "shabby ulster [coat], wearing a sorry looking derby hat, with a week's growth of beard, and shocking shoes." Indeed, the writer continued, he "looked rather like a mere stable attendant" instead of "the one-time Pooh-Bah of Independence, Iowa."

THE ARTICLE GOES on to provide the details of the decline of Williams' career. At the height of the trotting boom, he "had 'all kinds of money'…spent it liberally, built a kite-shaped race course…started a paper devoted to the horse, built a fine hotel [The Gedney], theatre, and bank in Independence, and tried to boom the town."

"But a pinch came, the boom collapsed, the newspaper suspended, real estate was a drug in the market, and everything, including the kite-shaped track and Independence itself, went by the board." When the dust had settled, "Williams was at the bottom of the wreck and completely crushed by it."

A view of Independence, Iowa, from Second Avenue Northeast looking south. Williams' Gedney Hotel and Opera House is on the left. Public domain.

Just a few years earlier, when Williams had been at the top of his game, one of his youthful employees had been a boy who loved working with horses, but wanted even more to become an artist. His name was William Edwards Cook, and in time he would leave Iowa to study art at schools in Chicago, New York and Paris. In Paris he became good friends with the American expatriate writer Gertrude Stein.

The first time that Cook attended a party at the famous apartment of Stein and her brother Leo, at 27 rue de Fleurus, he met another expatriate who was also attending a Stein soirée for the first time.

Her name was Alice B. Toklas, and she would soon become Gertrude Stein's partner. She was terribly nervous that night, and was ever so relieved to meet another American. When she asked Cook where he came from, and he replied "Independence, Iowa," she could hardly contain her excitement.

Toklas had grown up in California, but while she was young, Independence had often appeared in the national news, and she and Stein were well aware of the story of Williams' top stallions, Axtell and Allerton.

IT SEEMS THAT nearly everyone knew about Charles (known as C.W.) Williams, his horses and his kite-shaped track. As noted by a writer then, "Independence is a world-famed little city…[There is] No need now, when speaking of Independence, to add Iowa; everyone knows what is meant."

Williams sold Axtell to a syndicate for $105,000, equal to multi-millions now, the most ever paid for a race horse. Later, despite his and others' losses from an economic crash in 1892, he did not sell Allerton, but quietly rebuilt his wealth from the stallion's lucrative breeding fees.

Williams left Iowa in 1894, transported in eighteen railroad cars that carried his earthly belongings, and a string of fifty-four horses. He had been persuaded to move to Galesburg, Illinois (the site of the Lincoln-Douglas debate), where his success in horse racing and breeding continued.

He organized the Galesburg District Association, designed a brand new racetrack, and featured a new black mare named Alix, who was owned by a couple from Muscatine, Iowa, and who held the world trotting championship for six years, from 1894-1900. She acquired that distinction at Williams' track at Galesburg, which was not kite-shaped, but looked like a railroad coupling pin, with "dead level" parallel prongs.

DURING WILLIAMS' first year at Galesburg, among those working at the track was a stable hand and water boy, the son of Swedish immigrants, named Carl Sandburg.

He was not well-paid, but, as he recalled in his memoirs, "I had a pass to come in at any time and I saw up close the most famous trotting and pacing horses in the world, how they ran, and what the men were like who handled and drove them."

He also got to be around Charles Williams, if from a polite distance. "He was a medium-sized man with an interesting face," Sandburg remembered. "I thought his face looked like he had secrets about handling horses, yet past that there was a solemn look that bordered on the blank—I couldn't make it out."

The railway station and baggage area in Independence, Iowa. Public domain.

IN 1914, C.W. Williams was referred to in a news account as a "reformed race horse man," who had been converted to "old-time religion" after he having settled in Galesburg.

At some point, he traded all his horses in exchange for more than 33,000 acres of farmland in Saskatchewan in Canada. Once there, to visit all the farms he owned, he had to drive 350 miles. At the time, he was believed to be the largest individual grain farmer in North America.

Williams was now free to travel more, and he soon took up the part-time role of an itinerate evangelist—as Sandburg put it, he had hit "the sawdust trail"—speaking at churches in Galesburg and surrounding towns, while also returning to Iowa where he held revival meetings at Waterloo, Jesup, Independence, Des Moines, Cedar Rapids, and Mount Pleasant.

In 1925, three decades after moving from Independence to Galesburg, he moved to Aurora, Illinois, where he established a small stock farm for breeding registered cattle, which he called Axtell Herefords. He died there eleven years later, in February 1936.

In his autobiography, Carl Sandburg recalled the last time he saw Williams. It was on a passenger train from Chicago to Galesburg.

"He sat quiet in a seat by himself," remembered the poet, "And I could no more read his face than I could twenty years earlier. I like to think about him as I saw him once on an October morning, a little frost still on the ground, in a sulky jogging around the only dead level racetrack in the world, driving at a slow trot the stallion Allerton, being kind and easy with Allerton, whose speed was gone but whose seed were proud to call him grandsire." ■

HERBERT READ *The Contrary Experience*
Try as I would [as a child] I could not learn how to milk. To manipulate the teats so as to secure a swift and easy flow of milk demands a particular skill; I never acquired it, though my brothers, younger than I, seemed to find no difficulty. This was my first humiliation in the practical affairs of life; another which I might mention is an inability to make the kukkuk noise between the tongue and the palate which is the proper sound to urge a horse on gently.

THOMAS LOVE PEACOCK
Marriage may often be a stormy lake, but celibacy is almost always a muddy horse pond.

Portrait photograph of Samuel Franklin Cody (1909). Public domain. Library of Congress Prints and Photographs.

AIRBORNE VERSION
OF BUFFALO BILL

JONATHAN WINTERS

...when I was a kid, I shook hands with Orville Wright. Forty years later, I shook hands with Neil Armstrong. The guy that invented the airplane and the guy that walked on the moon.

OVER THE YEARS, I have often run across a photograph that is frequently mislabeled as a portrait of William Frederick Cody, famously known as Buffalo Bill. Whenever I see it, I can't help but do a double take: "That's not Bill Cody," I say to myself, "It can't be." Well, it does resemble him a bit, with cowboy hat, bandana, long hair, moustache, and goatee. But it's not him. The eyes, nose, ears and chin confirm that this is *not* the genuine Buffalo Bill.

Maybe it's one of his imitators? And there certainly were imitators: There were copycats who cashed in on his worldwide fame. They dressed like him, and gave performances like his, appearing in melodramas on stage or traveling around in bucking bronco Western shows.

There were also Buffalo Bill "doubles" who belonged to his own entourage, functioning when needed as "stand-ins" as the illustrious hero's health declined. One of those was a cowboy performer named Curt Alexander (originally from Leon, Iowa), whom I've talked about before. In early 1917, just two months after Buffalo Bill's funeral, while Alexander was visiting his nephew (a merchant who owned a clothing store in Cedar Falls), he spooked the local citizens when, attired in cowboy regalia, he was seen on downtown streets.

BUT THIS IS NOT Curt Alexander. No, the Cody look-alike in this photograph is yet another imitator, also an Iowan (from the Quad Cities, as was Cody himself) who, at birth, was christened Franklin Samuel Cowdery, but later switched to the modified name of Samuel Franklin Cowdery.

The real Buffalo Bill had been born in Le Claire in 1846, the year Iowa was granted statehood, whereas S.F. Cowdery was born in Davenport in 1867.

As a teenager, Cowdery moved to Montana, where he soon became adept at horseback riding, target shooting, and rope tricks. He would also later claim that he was born in Birdville, Texas, had survived an Indian raid during which his parents died, drove cattle on the Chisholm Trail, and prospected for gold in the Klondike, where he learned about how to build a kite from a Chinese cook.

In 1888, he joined a Western-themed traveling vaudeville troupe to perform as a trick roper, cowboy and marksman. It was also at around this time that he took on the surname of Cody, and was advertised as *Captain Cody, King of the Cowboys*. That same year, he also performed in Annie Oakley's touring show.

While on tour, he met a woman named Maude Lee, whom he married, and together they devised an act in which she assisted him in daring target shooting stunts. Aiming backwards through a mirror, he shot glass balls that she held up. Did Cowdery have any actual contact with the genuine Buffalo Bill? At least one source claims they met. But he did have unpleasant contacts with Cody's lawyers, who were on the lookout for fraudulent uses of Cody's name and the brand phrase Wild West.

IN 1890, WHEN Cowdery and Maude moved from the US to London, they joined a troupe that called itself the *Wild West Burlesque*, which Cody's lawyers soon closed down.

They then moved on to a different outfit, but made the mistake of billing themselves as *Captain Cody and Miss Cody: Buffalo Bill's Son and Daughter*. That too triggered legal alarms. Then the marriage to Maude began to dissolve. She moved on to other acts, somehow survived a parachute mishap, and ended up back in the US, where she died in an asylum.

Lithographic poster advertising daring bicycle racing acts. Public domain. Library of Congress Prints and Photographs.

Meanwhile, Cowdery fell in love with an older married equestrian named Lela Blackburne Davis, whose father was a wealthy horse breeder. She was fifteen years older than Cowdery and the mother of four children. In 1892, the unwed couple and their quasi-adopted children became *S.F. Cody and Family: Champion Shooters of America*.

They crossed the channel to perform in France. It was there that Cowdery learned about the frenetic popularity of bicycle racing. In addition to his popular sharpshooter performances, he began to challenge leading cyclists to contests in which he would race against them while riding on a horse. He inevitably won, and soon became known throughout Europe for his skills as an expert horseman.

IN 1898, Cowdery, Lela and their crew returned to England. It was also the year of the Spanish American War, and Cowdery began to consider the use (military and otherwise) of large scale observation kites.

His ideas were eventually a great success. He developed a man-lifting kite that could soar as high as 1000 feet, proposed experimental kites for the British War Office, and co-designed the first British airship or dirigible.

Colonel Samuel F. Cody at the controls of one of his early flying machines. Public domain.

In 1907, he set a world record for the longest airship flight, remaining aloft for three hours and twenty-five minutes. In the wake of that success—and in light of the rumors that the Wright brothers had successfully tested an airplane—Cowdery set about to devise his own powered aircraft.

He succeeded the following year, in what is now considered to be the first airplane flight in Britain. He soon became a national hero. Never again would he have to be known as Samuel Franklin Cowdery from Davenport, Iowa. He had completely morphed into Colonel Samuel Franklin Cody, the name by which he is known today.

It was Cowdery's daring that would also cause his tragic death. On August 7, 1913, he piloted a public demonstration flight of a new hydroplane, which he had designed for use in a future flying contest.

But something went wrong, and just as the plane was descending, parts of its fuselage pulled apart, the wings folded, and he and a celebrity passenger (neither of whom wore seatbelts in those days) died when they plunged to the ground from the sky. He was only forty-six.

ON THE DAY of Cowdery's fatal crash, the real Buffalo Bill Cody was still living, although he was in his mid-60s and troubled by declining health. He died four years later, on January 10, 1917. At his funeral service in Denver, Colorado, it was reported that those in attendance numbered around 20,000.

Had Colonel S.F. Cody (née Samuel Franklin Cowdery) been alive and in attendance at the funeral of Colonel William F. Cody, he might have felt some satisfaction to find that the crowd numbers at his own funeral in London were greater than those of Buffalo Bill.

The attendance at *his* service was 50,000. ■

CARL SANDBURG *Always the Young Strangers*
A Norwegian told me his mother sent him to a store to get something and he came home saying he forgot what she sent him for. She sent him again with the words, "What you don't keep in your head your feet must make up for, my little man." When he ate with his fingers and his grandmother told him to eat with his fork, he said, "Fingers were made before forks," and she cornered him, "But not your fingers."

Frank Lloyd Wright (1938), patent drawing for office chair. Public domain.

AN EDIFICE
TO EXPEDIENCY

ROGER G. BARKER Iowa-born psychologist
**We had a horse and buggy, cow, chickens, apple trees, a walnut grove,
a superior privy with three seats of different heights and sizes of
apertures.**

FRANK LLOYD WRIGHT and Grant Wood were assuredly *not* as
alike as "two peas in a pod." They differed in important ways.
And yet, as artists and designers, they had enough in common
that—metaphorically speaking—they might well be mistaken for
cousins.

Wright was born in rural Wisconsin in 1867. Like Wright,
Grant Wood was a quintessential Midwesterner. Born near
Anamosa, Iowa, in 1891, he was substantially younger than
Wright. At the time of Wood's birth, Wright was already well on
his way to becoming a prominent young architect in Chicago,
where he was the primary draftsman for Louis H. Sullivan, whom
he considered his mentor.

GRANT WOOD'S life ended early when he died of cancer one
day short of age 51 in 1942. Frank Lloyd Wright lived on for
many years. He was 91 when he died in 1959. All told, the two
co-existed in time for a half century, and, for a dozen or so of
those mutual years, they were both well-known Americans.
Surely, they were well aware of each other's celebrity, and yet, it
is remains unclear if they actually met.

Wood was reputed to be soft-spoken, affable and modest.
Wright was notoriously irascible, prone to making offensive

remarks. There is no doubt that Grant Wood was interested in architecture—after all, his best-known painting (*American Gothic*) pays homage, in part, to an architectural style. But if he had adverse opinions about Wright's architecture, they were apparently never recorded.

THERE WAS at least one documented occasion when Wood and Wright were in the same place at the same time—or at least, they were in the same city. In July 1939, both were invited to speak in Iowa City at a week-long Fine Arts Festival at the University of Iowa. At the time, Wood was on the faculty there, where he taught painting.

During that festival, he was scheduled to appear at a luncheon on Monday (the first event of the week). In addition, a dozen of his paintings, including *American Gothic* (never before shown in Iowa City), along with the work of other artists, were exhibited in the Iowa Union.

Frank Lloyd Wright was invited to give the final address at the close of the same festival. On Friday evening, he spoke to an outdoor crowd of about 1500 people on the west lawn of the Old Capitol building (which he tactlessly described as "a little old court house").

The following day, on Saturday morning, when Wright spoke publicly at a round table talk in the same building, he was introduced by the festival's organizer, who included an awkward disclaimer:

"Our visitor today said to me that he came to us as a physician comes to a patient. He did not come to praise, unless he found valid reason....And, as nearly as I can judge, he has found little....My own wish yesterday [in time spent with] this physician was that he would occasionally administer at least a mild anesthetic."

ONE WONDERS if Grant Wood attended Wright's talks at the festival. If so, he surely must have been dismayed by Wright's injurious comments.

According to Zella White Stewart (an actual physician), who witnessed both events, Wright "took a crack at [just] about everything." He dismissed the paintings on display as "art without a soul…[and thus evidence of] a lack of soul within the people."

In a news report that followed, he was quoted as describing the artworks as "painting–not art." Wright was, Zella Stewart continued, "the first visitor to tell us that Grant Wood's paintings were not a high form of art."

It is of interest that this Iowa City event took place about five weeks in advance of the invasion of Poland by Nazi Germany, an event that prompted World War II.

As Fascism gained the upper hand in Europe, Grant Wood was also under threat in Iowa, but for other reasons. Several members of the university community, who had been sowing suspicions about Grant Wood's sexual leanings, were also ardent advocates of Modern-era painting trends, and were intent on discrediting Wood.

He had studied art in Germany in the 1920s, and it was implied that his folksy Regionalist painting approach was somehow in lockstep with propagandistic figurative art, as championed by the Nazis.

OVER THE YEARS, quite a lot has been written about Wood's paintings in relation to his private life. They have been heavily harvested for hidden meanings.

At the moment, it is common to peruse his work in search of repressed erotic content, in which case pointy things are said to be sexual symbols, whereas other aspects are evidence of something else. Such speculation is engaging to a degree, but it can also be tenuous, as when camels and weasels appear in the clouds, as in Shakespeare's *Hamlet*.

Like those who see veiled implications in Grant Wood's compositions, Frank Lloyd Wright was himself adept at unearthing latent structures in otherwise seemingly innocent plans.

Among the best examples of this is a story that was told by one of Wright's associates, the architect Edgar Tafel in *About Wright*.

Tafel recalled that a committee from a certain church once met with Wright to discuss their requirements for a new worship facility. Wright agreed to produce a building plan, which he would present in a couple of weeks.

But Wright's studio staff was overwhelmed by other commissions, and they never found sufficient time to work on the church. As the deadline approached, Wright was advised by his staff to postpone the meeting with the church group, since the plans had not even been started.

Instead, at the very last minute, Wright pulled out of storage a set of abandoned building plans that he had drawn up for a small shopping center, a project that had fallen through.

ACCORDING TO Edgar Tafel, Wright replaced the labels for the shopping center spaces with new labels that would comply with the requirements of the church: "the [shopping center] bank became the [church] sanctuary, the supermarket became the Fellowship Hall, the [retail] stores [were instead identified as] classrooms, and on and on."

By the time the church committee arrived, the set of plans had been renamed, "and Mr. Wright showed them the drawings, with accustomed gusto and aplomb."

At the end of Wright's presentation, "the pastor said: 'Lord, we thank thee for leading us to a great architect, who has designed, in your honor, an edifice we will use and enjoy. Amen.'" ■

MARK VAN DOREN *Autobiography*

He loved to call things by the wrong names—or, it may be, the right ones, fantastically the right ones. Either extreme is poetry, of which he had the secret without knowing that he did. It was natural for him to name two lively rams on the place Belshazzar and Nebuchadnezzar ... [Mark's brother] Frank became Fritz Augustus—just why, I never inquired and I was either Marcus Aurelius or Marco Bozzaris. Guy was Guy Bob, and Carl was Carlo. And Paul, when it came time for him to share in the illicit luxuriance, was no other than Wallace P. Poggin. Again, I have no faint idea why. My father never discussed his inspirations, any more than he analyzed his spoonerisms, or even admitted that they had fallen from his mouth. He would cough, and appear to apologize by saying: "I have a little throakling in my tit."

GRETA SERGEANT *recalling A.S. Neill*

Once he visited a school in Stockholm, and was taken in to a geography lesson. He went up to the map on the wall, pointed to Italy, and said: "This is London."

Author's montage from public domain components

FLOTSAM ADRIFT IN
A MADDENING CROWD

QUENTIN CRISP The Naked Civil Servant
The young always have the same problem: how to rebel and conform at the same time.

AS A HIGH SCHOOL student in Iowa, I was an avid follower of MAD Magazine. I also subscribed to the *Village Voice* and the *New York Review of Books*. Concerned about my waywardness, my mother arranged for me to meet with a religious elder for an advisory conversation.

I was a youthful artist then, and during that meeting the subject turned to visual art. The sagacious elder said to me that, only that morning, he had read an editorial in the *Wall Street Journal* that proclaimed that "Modern Art is a dung heap."

Moments later, I was somewhat put at ease when he laughed good-naturedly and said that it was his opinion that there was no reason for anyone to worry about me—I was going through a youthful phase.

Most likely, the source of my problem, he said, was that I was reading "too much MAD Magazine." Out of politeness, I didn't respond. But in my mind I wondered if the source of *his* problem was that he was reading "too much *Wall Street Journal*."

I RECALL THAT a further concern at the time was my new-found interest in the Beat Generation and in writers referred to as "beatniks." A few years earlier, a former football player from Lowell, Massachusetts, named Jack Kerouac (one of whose high school classmates had been comedian Ray Goulding of the hilarious *Bob and Ray* radio comedy team) had published a rambling, unorthodox novel called *On the Road*.

Among my chief interests was literature, controversial or not. I had first read Kerouac's book around 1962, including that now-famous passage in which he lamented having traveled through Iowa too quickly—"past the pretty girls, and the prettiest girls in the world live in Des Moines."

When *On the Road* was first released in 1957, reactions from critics were radically mixed. As its notoriety spread, so did the fame of its author, who soon became referred to as the King of the Beats. His book was a pivotal influence on a generation of writers, musicians, and others, among them the Beatles, David Bowie, Bob Dylan, Jim Morrison, and photographer Robert Frank.

Debate about Kerouac's novel increased exponentially when it was revealed that the book had been typed on a continuous 120-foot scroll of tracing paper, single-spaced, without any paragraph breaks, much less breaks for chapters.

The author referred to this approach as "spontaneous prose," but Truman Capote was unconvinced: What Kerouac does, said Capote, "is not writing—it's typing."

CONCURRENT WITH this, another leading figure in the Beat Generation, a New York poet named Allen Ginsberg, had published a lengthy protest poem called *Howl*. Initially banned as being obscene, it was cleared in a famous court case in 1957, the year that *On the Road* came out.

This was followed two years later by William S. Burrough's *The Naked Lunch*, also condemned as being obscene, and in turn, this trinity of infamy—Kerouac, Ginsberg, and Burroughs—became widely recognized as the "beatific" echelon.

To my memory, the most enduring of the three was Ginsberg, no doubt partly because of the fact that, in the spring of 1968, when I was an undergraduate at the State College of Iowa (now the University of Northern Iowa), he was invited to visit the campus for three days. During his visit, I was able to speak to him briefly, and to be present at two of his readings.

TO UNDERSTAND WHY Ginsberg was of interest then to myself and other students, it is essential to realize that, at the time, public protests against the Vietnam War were occurring nationwide. He had been invited to speak on numerous campuses, and was widely recognized as one of the war's most virulent critics.

The campus at Cedar Falls was especially poised for a rally by a rousing war opponent. Only a few months earlier, one of the school's English professors had publicly burned his draft card. In response, there was an outcry from community "patriots," who demanded that the school's president, J.W. Maucker, should fire the protesting teacher, although he had not yet been charged or convicted.

And, if Maucker failed in doing that, then he himself should be dismissed. Among students, there was a remarkable show of support for Maucker's defense of due process, and freedom of speech, including opposing the Vietnam War.

The degree of support is confirmed by a clipping from the *Des Moines Register* (dated October 21, 1967) in which there is photograph of myself (as one of the protest enablers), holding a petition for students to sign. The news article states that an estimated 5,000 students signed that document during a rally one evening. We then marched to Maucker's home, to stand in vigil throughout the night.

ANOTHER LESS EVIDENT factor was that the country was still in the process of healing its self-inflicted wounds from the so-called American "Red Scare," an anti-Communist witch hunt that had been spearheaded by Wisconsin senator Joseph McCarthy from 1947 to 1957.

Not only did McCarthy seek to "out" Communists, Socialists, or simply political liberals, he also ran a side campaign, known as the "Lavender Scare," in which he and others searched for government employees who might be gay, for the purpose of demanding that they be terminated.

As a result, Ginsberg had multiple reasons for speaking out against demagogues, since he himself was openly gay. In addition, his mother, a Jewish-Russian emigré, had been an active Marxist, who sometimes took her sons along when she attended political meetings.

Following a breakdown, she was institutionalized for mental illness, including the "delusion" that the FBI was watching her—which was, most likely, well-founded. As is commonly noted, even if clinically paranoid, it doesn't mean that someone is not being followed.

IN THE DAYS before his appearance in Cedar Falls, Ginsberg had spoken in Appleton, Wisconsin, at Lawrence University. His Wisconsin visit made national news, because Appleton was Joe McCarthy's hometown, and, before leaving town, he and his followers gathered at McCarthy's grave, where they performed what they described as a urine-based ceremonial rite to release McCarthy's demons.

Arriving at the Waterloo airport, Ginsberg spoke at a press conference. He was then escorted to campus, where, for the next few days, he spoke publicly, performed at poetry readings, and visited on-going classes.

Among those classes was a drawing class in the Arts and Industries Building, in which I was enrolled. He had a great full beard, and the drawing instructor suggested that Ginsberg simply sit on a chair on a platform, so that the students could draw him.

I did this for a few minutes, but it soon occurred to me that I was missing an opportunity. So I suddenly stood up, walked over to him, sat on the floor in front of him, and the two of us began to talk. I recall almost nothing of our conversation, except for one vivid exception: I remember that he told me about having recently witnessed a film being made beneath the Brooklyn Bridge, based on a script by Irish playwright Samuel Beckett, and featuring Buster Keaton.

I saw Ginsberg later a couple of times, but I remember almost no details. I recall that I attended an evening party, organized by students, that was held in adjacent apartments (the doors had been opened to create a single, continuous space) at a large historic building located at Fourth and Main in downtown Cedar Falls. It was extremely crowded.

There was a less dense gathering at an off-campus coffee house, during which he chanted as he accompanied himself with a small red box-like portable accordion.

I sat back and took it in, but there were aspiring writers who passed him scraps of paper, with their contact information and examples of their poetry, in the hope that he might "discover" their talents after he left.

MY FINAL, MOST lasting memory is that of being in the audience when he gave a major reading in the Auditorium of what is now Lang Hall (where Salvador Dali had given a talk in 1952). I was seated in the balcony on the right, from which I had an excellent view.

The highlight of the evening came when he read one of his most compelling works, titled "Wichita Vortex Sutra" in a forceful, rhythmic voice. Written in 1966, it was a poem about the Vietnam War that he had composed while traveling through Kansas on a bus.

Whenever I think of that reading by Ginsberg, it inevitably brings to mind an earlier, equally powerful talk that I had attended one year earlier—on the same campus, same building, and in the same auditorium.

It was one of the last public lectures by an old charismatic champion of freedom of speech, American Socialist Norman Thomas. He was in his early 80s and all but impossibly hampered by old age, arthritis, and declining vision. In advance of his speech, it appeared that they might have to carry him to the front, and prop him up his arms on the lectern. But once so positioned, a powerful, clarion voice broke out, and took command of all the seats.

Norman Thomas soon retired from public life. He died in late 1968, at age 86, just a few months after Ginsberg's talk.

As a perennial candidate for the US Presidency, this tall, handsome, courageous hero had always been well-spoken, and was known for his witty rejoinders.

While confirming that he was encouraged to see a new generation of outspoken youth—alluding to beatniks and others—he said, "I just wish they'd cut their hair." ■

END MATTER

GEORGE MOORE *The Brook Kerith*
**A man travels the world in search of what he needs
and returns home to find it.**

SINCE IOWA is the common thread that runs throughout these essays, what could be more appropriate than to disclose that, without exception, all the essays in this book have been published previously, in the past several decades, in magazines published in the state.

Of foremost importance is *The Iowa Source* (a magazine published in Fairfield, Iowa) in which most of the essays first appeared, albeit with somewhat different wording and with different headings.

That magazine was founded forty years ago by Claudia Mueller, who continues as its editor. My experience in working with her and the magazine's staff could not have been more pleasurable. I am grateful for their efforts.

A small number of the remaining essays (perhaps two or three) first appeared in a short-lived intereesting magazine, published in Cedar Rapids, called *Tractor: Iowa Arts and Culture*.

WHEREVER I HAVE lived, I could not help but wonder what has taken place, in the same location, in the decades and centuries prior to mine. While living in Iowa, I have often benefited from the collections (and recollections) of my brother, Richard H. Behrens, who has an avid interest in the history of the American

Midwest, and especially in our family's past. Without his input, I may not have been able to tell the story of our paternal grandfather's death ("Holding Down the Fort's Remains"), our maternal ancestors' connection to the Navajo trading posts in New Mexico ("Living Among the Navajo"), or the dream-like meteoric rise of Iowa race track entrepreneur Charles Williams in the distant past of our hometown ("Horse Racing's One-Time Pooh-Bah").

My own interests tend to be Laocoön-like. While this book is about Iowa, *not* about camouflage (which I am too often known for writing about), at least two of the essays provide accounts of the contributions to WWI camouflage of two Iowa artists, Sherry Edmundson Fry and Carol Mayer Sax ("Sherry Fry and the Birth of Camouflage" and "Ottumwa's Theatrical Ship Camoufleur," respectively).

Nor is it a book about Buffalo Bill Cody. Or sand painting. Or Native Americans. Or Frank Lloyd Wright. Or dreams. Or Dada and Surrealism, or book design. And yet I can't prevent those themes from rising to the surface, like irrepressible volunteer plants that yearn for the warmth of the sun above, like it or not.

As in everything I do, I am especially indebted to the love and boundless devotion of my wonderful wife and companion, Mary Snyder Behrens. What would I do without her? —RB

ABOUT THE AUTHOR

Until his retirement in 2018, **Roy R. Behrens** was Professor of Art and Distinguished Scholar at the University of Northern Iowa. He had taught graphic design and design history there and at other universities and art schools for more than 45 years. He is the author of seven books, and literally hundreds of articles in journals, books, and magazines, and has appeared in broadcast interviews on NOVA, National Public Radio, Australian Public Radio, BBC, and Iowa Public Television, as well as in documentary films. He has been a nominee for the Smithsonian's National Design Awards, has received the Pushcart Prize, the Iowa Board of Regents Faculty Excellence Award, and has been described in *Communication Arts* magazine as "one of the most original thinkers in design."

OTHER BOOKS BY THE SAME AUTHOR

1977 (with Jerome Klinkowitz) *The life of fiction*. University of Illinois Press. ISBN 978-0252006432. **1981** *Art & camouflage: Concealment and deception in nature, art and war*. North American Review / University of Northern Iowa. ISBN 978-0915996070. **1984** *Design in the visual arts*. Prentice-Hall. ISBN 978-0132019477. **1986** *Illustration as an art*. Prentice-Hall. ISBN 978-0134514284. **2002** *False colors: Art, design and modern camouflage*. Bobolink Books. ISBN 978-0971324404. **2005** *Cook book: Gertrude Stein, William Cook and Le Corbusier*. Bobolink Books. ISBN 978-0971324411. **2009** *Camoupedia: A compendium of research on art, architecture, and camouflage*. Bobolink Books. ISBN 978-0971324466. **2012** *Ship shape: a dazzle camouflage sourcebook*. Bobolink Books. ISBN 978-0971324473. **2016** *Frank Lloyd Wright and Mason City: Architectural heart of the prairie*. History Press. ISBN 978-1467118606. ■

RELATED ONLINE SOURCES

PUBLISHER'S
WEBSITE

UNIVERSITY
SCHOLARWORKS

AUTHOR'S
WEBSITE

POETRY OF
SIGHT BLOG

AUTHOR'S
VIDEO TALKS

CAMOUPEDIA
BLOG

AUTHOR'S
PUBLICATIONS

WIKIPEDIA
BIOGRAPHY